The Evolution Of Self

MY PAIN, YOUR FREEDOM

Jordan M. Author

To my fabulous five—Erica, Jaelyn, Amayah, Hailey and Zayn: I love you. In a world full of chaos and grief, you guys make me feel whole again. Family is everything, and with all I've built and accomplished, none of it would mean anything without you all.

To you, Mom, the matriarch of our family: With all the words in this book, there still aren't enough words to express how much I love you.

And last but not least, a letter to heaven. Thank you, Nee Naw. You remain the comforting voice that serves as my constant reminder: I can still hear you saying, "I'm proud of you, baby."

Contents

CHAPTER 1

A Dollar and a Dream... But Without the Dollar

Normally birthdays don't make you feel any different. From the time I turned eight years old, people would ask me, "How does it feel to be eight now?" or "How does it feel to be eighteen?" Usually, I answered: "It feels the same." But not this time. It felt totally different and quite satisfying. That day, I turned twenty-one years old. Twenty-one is like your sweet sixteen all over again but for adults. The highly anticipated day of every teenager's life! You're finally twenty-one years old and can legally drink alcohol. You can now go into any and every bar with your head held high and a straight back knowing you'll be served as you proudly show off your new ID as a badge of honor. You can sit down with your parents at any restaurant, order your favorite alcoholic beverage, and act like it's your first time trying it, even though you've been "tasting" alcohol since you were eighteen or younger.

But just say you're not a drinker; turning twenty-one is still such a big deal. Why? Because you no longer have to sit at the kids table at family functions. From that day forward, you command respect as you happily march right up to the "grown folks" table and join in on conversations that are usually about recent life successes or petty family gossip. Most times, when people celebrate their twenty-first birthday, they plan to go to the clubs, bars, or some venue that provides an opportunity for an immense amount of drinking and partying until you black out and forget what you did from the time you entered the club until you left. But not me.

That day was the day that everything we'd been planning for six months was made manifest. For my twenty-first birthday I combined my birthday celebration with the launch of my brand "McCook&Co." This party was going to be different and daring. I wanted to make this an experience, something to be remembered. Without having an enormous budget to work with, I'd have to be extremely frugal when spending but still make this event a jaw-dropping experience. The creative juices began to seep from my pores as I searched for unique ways to combine entertainment and excellence to my twenty-first birthday while at the same time launching my brand.

Leading up to that day, I planned and strategized with some close friends as to how I would bring this vision to fruition. First things first, I needed a venue that could hold all the people I planned to invite. We spent weeks looking at different venues around the city that could accommodate exactly what we were looking for and within my budget. I didn't know anything about party planning, and I wasn't sure where I would get the resources to make it happen. Hell, I had just graduated high school a couple years prior and now I was planning an elaborate event to have all my friends and family share in the launch of my brand. So the question was: how was I going to be able to pull this one off?

For about fifteen months I'd been saving $1000 a month from the money I earned at my job at a local barber shop which bridged the gap between old school and new school. After solidifying a venue costing almost $1000, one month's savings, I focused on finding and executing ideas that would make this event stand out! I needed something to give my celebration a wow factor.

Now where was I going to get the money to be able to pull off a WOW?

By the time I turned twenty-one, I woke up each morning living in my two-bedroom bachelor pad and driving my blue Pontiac G6, which I bought, paid in full from my savings. It was a 2007 Pontiac G6, so it was nine years old, but I kept it clean. (If you know, you know.) It was one of my most prized possessions at the time. I'd always heard the quote, "I've got a dollar and a dream" which was a cute thing to say, but coming out of high school, I didn't even have that. All I had was a dream. After graduating, I'd dedicated and committed myself to barbering and becoming the best at it. It would've been nice to have Mommy and Daddy fund this celebration, or to have received an inheritance to pay for this party, but that wasn't the case. The hustle of barbering was responsible for this bill.

I checked off my checklist the things I wanted to see at this celebration. I needed a backdrop with my company's logo printed on it for pictures. I needed lights for the stage and for the venue to create the proper ambiance. An extravagant meal and dessert were necessary for my guests, so hiring a top chef to cater this event was essential. This was going to be a black-and-white affair, so standing out from the crowd was a nonnegotiable. I had to have the flyest outfit.

I needed someone to capture all of this on video for the world to see, so I hired the best videographer and photographer, Joseph, who was known around the city for filming and editing the dopest video productions. But this was a brand launch and I couldn't stop there. I needed merchandise to sell. I jumped on the phone with a friend from Houston, Johnny P. JP was a recording artist who had many connections is his city. He'd worked with a wholesaler to order clothing for his own brand and I knew he could fulfill this order of one hundred shirts for my party guest. Each shirt had the McCook&Co. logo in three different colors, black, white and gold. Having something at the merchandise table to represent my innovation as a barber was also imperative. After watching many DIY YouTube videos, my two younger sisters, Jaelyn and Amayah, and I became product manufacturers by creating our own hair products out of my apartment kitchen to sell at the brand launch party.

Everything was coming together so smoothly but we still needed the entertainment. From networking at different church functions, I gathered five of the best artists and musicians from around Texas to perform at this grand event, talent ranging from poets to saxophone players to entire jazz bands. This event was going to be monumental and I was here for it.

With party guests pouring in, I chose to follow proper protocol of being fashionably late to make my grand entrance! As I made my way to the entrance, I was greeted at the door with big smiles from my closest homies who acted as my "security." We didn't actually need security, but why not? They knew how hard I had worked for this day. This was my moment and everything was going according to plan. Door ticket sales were flooding, (yes, I charged to get in my party) and the support from merchandise sales was heartwarming. The food was superb and the live band was even better. Each poet delivered with a heartfelt passion and the audience looked on in awe. As the celebration progressed, I kept finding myself standing on the back wall, watching it all in disbelief. I couldn't believe the support from my friends and family as they all made this occasion memorable.

The success of my party seemed like the climax of turning twenty-one years old, but as the year progressed, so did my career. I was invited to perform my first ever celebrity haircut. Later that same day, I entered my first ever barber battle where I competed and took home a surprising prize. I began traveling around my city conducting inspirational shows and establishing a name for myself. That progressed into having my own radio show with over 100,000 listeners every week. I became the youngest and only barber in the state of Texas to have a radio show on the airwaves. That year, I also appeared on stage at a major festival and opened my first brick-and-mortar business.

My personal life, also underwent a major transformation. In September of that same year, I stood in a flood of emotions as I watched my son being born. From that day on, I was never the same. Fatherhood awakened me to a world of love that I had never experienced in my life. And I was instantly consumed and appreciative of every moment with him. I felt invincible as we beat the drum again for the grand opening of my business the following month. This was everything I could hope for and felt larger than life. Within that same year I started the process to purchase my first house.

I was creating everything I said I wanted. Yet something was missing.

I was a multi-award winning barber and an inspirational speaker and educator. I had multiple successful business ventures. Yet, I still felt a void in my heart. An emptiness. I was making six-figures doing work I loved. I was a constant presence in the life of a son who I loved more than I knew was possible. I was using my gift as a barber to reach people in new ways. So why was there this unfillable hole in my soul?

CHAPTER 2

Eden Has Mice

Dave Chappelle said, in his stand-up comedy special on Netflix, "My parents did just well enough so that I could grow up poor around white people!" Hilarious. Well, Dave, my experience wasn't much different. 6524 Fairdale Drive, a three-bedroom townhouse, was the placed we called home, the place where it all began. The only boy of four children, I was raised in a single-parent household by a strong and independent mother, who made sure we lacked for nothing. At the time, my older sister, Erica, and Mom were all I knew. They were my whole world.

Erica and I looked forward to the simple pleasures only small children understand, like trying to remember and recite the theme song to Sponge Bob Square Pants when it premiered in May of 1999. She and I were insep-arable. See, Erica was my voice of reason, the coolest big sister a little brother could ask for. Being four years older than I, her peculiar imagination opened my mind to a world full of color and adventures. She was always up to something, and I was right on her heels. We cried together, laughed together, and explored together.

On days when Mom didn't drop us off at school, Erica and I walked. Leaving the house, the chill from the night greeted us at the door. The morning dew was still on the grass, and there was a slight fog in the air. The road was quiet this early in the morning, and the only voices echoing down the street were Erica's and mine. We played a game Erica created, called the Safari. Our imaginations took us to the southern plains of Africa as we left the house, making our way to school. "Jordan look!" Erica shouted. "There's a giraffe over there eating." And at just four years old, I gazed in awe at the blinking yellow school-zone sign as if a twenty-foot-tall giraffe was having breakfast from the trees that dangled over the sidewalk. As we walked on, the jungle slowly faded and became our school.

Erica was creative and far more daring than I. She never feared much and was willing to take risks with our explorations that sometimes took us to uncharted territory. Mom often erupted about us always "being into something." When she did, it was every man for himself. When the belt came out, Erica was a runner. One day, Erica tossed fake grass from a plant in the house on Mom as she stepped fresh out the shower. The grass rained down like confetti, sticking to Mom's body as she let out a shriek of disbelief. After realizing that was a mistake, Erica tried to escape, but she ran face first into the corner of a dresser, splitting her cheek open.

What would possess Erica to do such a thing to our Mom? The world may never know. But in her mind, it made sense. I told you, she wasn't afraid of much, and quite frankly, still isn't. Minus Candyman. Any child growing up in the '90s knew of Candyman. To this day, I wouldn't dare say "Candyman" three times in a mirror. Why? Because I thoroughly enjoy the life I live and wouldn't jeopardize it by causing some slasher with a hook for a hand to appear in my house.

Erica was almost fearless, but from an early age, I decided to be a lot more conservative with the decisions I made. Every move was calculated. I had to see each stair before taking a step. Truth is I was scary. Plain and simple. Terrified of my own shadow. The world talks about having anxiety now, but I was the definition of anxiety back then. The smallest things terrified me. It didn't take much to have me in a full-blown cry, as if the world was ending. Bugs, animals, thunder and lightning, or sometimes people—yes, some people simply terrified me.

I don't have a logical explanation why I was scared of everything, but my constant fears meant I stuck to my mother like glue. She was raised on the South Side of Chicago and was tougher than a junkyard dog. She was my protector, my provider, my lifeline that would show up in my time of need. Mom was Mufasa, and I was Simba. She comforted me, in her arms I felt at ease. I always wanted to be up under my mom. I'm a mama's boy at heart. She was the only parent I had, but even if my dad was around, I still would've chosen Mom.

I was the type of child who constantly needed affection, to be reaffirmed in love, and Mom did that. Some nights, she, Erica, and I all fell asleep on the same couch, Erica at one end and me tangled in Mom's arms. This went on even while my mom was pregnant with Jaelyn, my younger sister. We'd all pile on the couch and totally ignore the fact that there were four perfectly good beds upstairs in our rooms. But she was mama bear and we were her cubs, innocent and safe in the presence of our comforter.

Fairdale Drive was the extent of the world I knew and possessed all I needed, like my own Garden of Eden. It wasn't the projects, but it for damn sure wasn't the Hamptons either. Our townhome was located next to a huge field, where new developments were still being built. One evening, when mom made her way home, she heard scurrying in our walls, a ruffling sound that captivated our ears and alarmed us. We questioned, for days, what could be causing all the noise. Mom wasn't a fan of the unwanted critters infiltrating our utopia. She believed they'd come from the family we shared a wall with, who had recently moved in.

One day, racing to play in our back yard, then making our way to the garage, Erica and I heard a ruffling noise. "Jordan! Grab a box!" screamed Erica. "For what?" I asked. Hesitant, I peeked around the corner and finally saw what was causing all the commotion. Mice! Erica was fascinated and I—well, I was scared stiff. But I followed her courage. "They'll be our pets!" Erica said, and I agreed. Whether they were field mice that came from the vacant lot of land next to our townhomes or from the new family next door didn't matter to us.

As evening hit, Mom came home from work and we bombarded her with stories from our day as she walked through the door. Little did she know, we'd just acquired our two new pets, but we were so excited to show her our little surprises. "Mom, come to the garage! We've got something to show you!" I said. As we raced out the back door, following the trail to the garage, my mother's countenance fell. She didn't like it.

"Look Mom! Our new pets!" said Erica. Mom jumped back in shock. "Get those damn rats out of my house!

Now!" She shouted. She'd never been a fan of animals of any sort and to make rodents pets was the last thing on her mind. We were innocent and figured, if we surprised her with our new pets, she'd lets us keep them. Not a cat, nor a stray puppy, rats. The imaginative mind of a five-year-old and nine-year-old. I told you this wasn't the Hamptons.

* * *

One morning, we were all rushing to get out of the house. Running late after losing track of time, we zipped through the backyard and to the garage. I always wanted to push the button that opened the garage door, so I begged and pleaded with my sister to let me do it. She lifted me up to do so and as the door went up, my mother realized she'd forgotten her makeup bag in the house. She settled us in the car and ran back to the house to grab the bag.

While we waited for our mom, a navy blue pickup truck pulled up and parked right behind our car. A man got out and approached our car, and my sister raced to the house to alert Mom of what was taking place. He was still making his way to our car when mother returned, screaming and shouting at the man. He quickly ran back to his truck and fled. I had no idea what was going on, but I was afraid. I could tell Mom was livid, but none of the emotions made sense to me. She jumped in our car with us and followed him as he darted through the streets trying to lose us. After we'd followed him for some time, he made his way to his house where she pulled directly in front of his house to confront him. He ran inside so Mom called the police, but without a witness, there was nothing they could do.

Mom later explained that the man had seen two kids alone and thought he could snatch one or both of us. That day and throughout that time, she did such an amazing job shielding us from the very present dangers that existed all around us. She juggled being our nurturer and our hedge of protection. Where our fathers were supposed to step in and be our security, our provision , she handled it and did it well.

Mom was thriving at a company where she'd worked for many years, MCI WorldCom. She was making about $50,000 a year, a lot of money back then, especially for someone who hadn't gone to college. Times were good. and Mom decided we should take a family trip to Disney World for Erica's tenth birthday. I was about six years old, and my baby sister, Jaelyn, was just two. Our family of four traveled with a close friend of the family and her children on a Greyhound bus headed to Orlando, Florida.

On the way, we encountered a horrific storm, and rain pouring out of the sky impaired the bus driver's vision. Squinting to just see a couple feet ahead of us, he had no idea that traffic had come to a complete stop. Out of nowhere, the bus, carrying more than fifty passengers, slammed into the back of standstill traffic causing the massive bus to jerk off the road roll onto the side of an embankment. Within seconds of the crash, Mom clutched all three of us from our seats and into her arms and began to pray. All I could hear were the wails and screaming of people on the bus, everyone terrified.

A moment of silence hushed the bus as we all froze in fear of what was to come next. Then, everyone scrambled to the right side of the bus to balance the weight and prevent us from flipping over and down the steep hill. We huddled there until the fire department could fight through traffic to get to us. I was in utter disbelief to see one mother jump out the window of the bus leaving her young daughter aboard. A man dressed in his navy uniform shouted and hollered, demanding the bus driver let him off the bus. He explained his father had died while he was deployed. He was on the way to the funeral and couldn't miss it. But all we could do was wait. No sudden movements were allowed as we remained stiff, attempting to not tumble to our deaths.

The fire department eventually made their way to us, wrapped their hoses around the windows of the bus, and pulled us back to stable ground. Once we were able to get off the bus safely, we were met by news cameras and reporters.

We spent the night in a Greyhound station, states away from home, sleeping on rock-hard waiting chairs. What was supposed to be a glorious time at "the happiest place on Earth" had become a nightmare.

CHAPTER 3

Trail of Storms

Maya Angelou once wrote, "We delight in the beauty of the butterfly, but rarely admit the changes it has gone through to achieve that beauty." I felt that. There's this weird correlation between pain and beauty. It's almost as if you can't have one without the other. Yin and yang. A caterpillar must suffer an intense metamorphosis before ever experiencing life as a majestic butterfly. If we want to evolve, we must experience similar suffering. There's no other way to experience this evolution other than to go through it. You can't go around it, you can't go over it, and you can't skip it. You must go through it. Change is inevitable. Change is constant. But yet, growth is optional. We have to choose it, and the hardest part about growing is you can't feel the movement.

A shift was happening as we prepared to pack up and move into a new house. In February of 2002, we made the transition. New neighborhood, new schools, new friends, and a new house. It was an exciting time for my sisters and I, as we always appreciated new things. Besides, this house was significantly different from what we would always call "the old house." It was like a mansion to us, ten steps above our previous living situation. It was new construction, and we were the first ones to live there. The thrill of being able to pick out our rooms was invigorating. Not only did we each have our own space, but there was also a game room where we planned to have heaps of fun.

When we moved, some of my mother's friends and coworkers helped us paint and decorate the house. Mom's friends became like family to us. They were all so loving and kind to my sisters and I. Their energy was contagious. They were the type of people who could start a party any and everywhere.

During this time, the company my mother worked for was rocked by a huge scandal. In June of 2002 the CEO was convicted of fraud and sentenced to twenty-five years in prison. While he paid a price, the employees of MCI WorldCom did too. Along with thousands of people, my mom was laid off from the job that had provided security and comfort for us. Our family was completely blindsided and never saw this coming.

All sharing in the same tragedy, Mom's co-workers still came around, or we'd travel once a year to the beach and meet up with them. One friend came around a lot more often than the others. Her name was Keera, and we called her Miss Keera. She'd attend all the city festivals and carnivals with us, and she was tons of fun. Miss Keera was easy-going and always kept a smile on her face. I can't recall ever seeing her angry. As months went on, Erica and I noticed a closeness between my mother and Miss Keera. She eventually moved into the house with us and quickly became like family.

Erica and I weren't bothered at all by Miss Keera moving in. Our needs were taken care of at home and she was good company. Miss Keera fit right in, dancing around the house, recording us with her camcorder as Jaelyn and I performed impromptu dance routines. She cooked, cleaned, and helped out around the house, filling in the holes where my mom couldn't, financially and sometimes emotionally. We were happy.

Out of the blue, Mom gathered us kids together one day to ask us how we felt about having another sibling. We stood there puzzled, scratching our heads and questioning what life would be like with a fourth child running around the house with us. We'd gotten so used to things being the way they were it was hard to imagine another sibling. I already had two sisters, so my only request was that it be a boy. I wanted a brother badly. Someone to wrestle with, play sports with, share in troubles with, and bond with. Mom went on to explain that a relative of Miss Keera was having a baby, who we would adopt as our own. I guess we didn't have much of a say-so on this matter anyway, but she ran it by us just to see our reactions.

Miss Keera's family was from Tulsa, Oklahoma, and we drove nine hours to get there. The trip was nothing short of amazing. We played road-trip games nonstop. At one point, Jaelyn and I had so much fun making up songs and twirling round and round in the back seat that we eventually tangled ourselves in our seatbelts. I was able to break free but she was stuck. Like for real stuck. Being claustrophobic, she began to panic, and I laughed until my stomach hurt. Mom, on the other hand, didn't find this funny at all. She pulled the SUV over on the side of the highway, got out, and came around and whooped Jaelyn untangled. It was still funny, but laughing wasn't an option.

All the fun came to a halt when my mom finally disclosed the gender of our new sibling. "It's a girl!" she yelled. Overtaken with emotion, I burst into tears. I broke down and threw the biggest tantrum, screaming and shouting, "I just want a brother!" My display was comical to my mother and Miss Keera, but I was completely distraught. Whether I liked it or not, we were getting a new baby sister, Amayah.

We arrived at the hospital the same day Amayah was born, and after spending almost a week in Tulsa, we brought our little sister home to San Antonio. Though I cried when I found out she was a girl, after holding her and locking eyes with her, our bond was set for life. She's never felt like my adopted sister. She always fit right in, and I cherished my new baby sister.

Around this time, a rift developed in our household. I couldn't comprehend everything taking place, but I knew something was off. After less than a year of living with us, Miss Keera moved out and stopped coming around. She had been a major influence in my life and had played the role of a second parent for me. She was a tomboy type, rough around the edges, and for a young boy without a man in the house, she had been someone relatable. Unfortunately, her relationship with my mom was over, and she was gone.

* * *

Erica and I occasionally attended church with our maternal grandmother, Nee-Naw. It was like a little vacation away from home that we looked forward to every week. By the end of church on Sunday, we couldn't tell you what the pastor preached about, but we looked forward to going out to eat afterwards. Our favorite spot was Luby's. They served home-style, comfort food that satisfied our souls. And hanging out with Nee-Naw was always a heartwarming time.

Nee-Naw was the best example of Christ Jesus in our eyes. She loved the homeless just as she loved royalty. She never discriminated, and made each of us and everyone we saw her come in contact with feel loved and welcomed. Her heart was so big. She made everyone feel like family, and she especially loved her family. Nee-Naw was a very wise woman. Having experienced her own share of life's ups and down, she'd share endless words of wisdom that could radiate the soul of any individual. But it wasn't simply her wisdom, it was her unique ability to meet you where you were and share a love that only your mother could give. An agape love. And I was proud to call her my grandmother.

Erica eventually developed her own faith and attended church regularly with Nee-Naw. This was her safe space. Her home away from home. She'd come back home and teach me the stories and principles taught to her. Her stories never really struck my interest until she came home talking about a new term, "age of accountability." At eleven years old, my sister explained, I'd have to take responsibility for my actions and give an account for my sins. I had no idea what sins were, and the thought scared the hell right out of me. I had no clue about my soul's salvation. The idea that there was an age at which God expected me to take responsibility for my sins totally caught me off guard.

I had so many questions. What are sins? What did I do wrong? What's going to happen if I don't repent? My eyes were opened. I'd never heard of this man called Jesus and certainly didn't know he was God. I had to see what all the talk was about. After many late nights of Erica going over basic Bible stories with me, I had enough. I wanted to attend this church to figure it all out for myself. She explained to me that church had much more to offer than just going out to eat afterward. The next Sunday I went to church and, for the first time, I paid attention. I soaked in every word that fell from the pastor's lips. I didn't want to be lost. I wanted to be saved! My moral compass and belief system were being shaped, and I began to see the world through a different lens.

With everything I learned at church, I began taking account for my spirituality and concerning myself with salvation. I went to church more often, and my relationship with God and knowledge about my faith really grew. Going to church gave me a foundation for my beliefs and so my heart was burdened by the things of

God at a very young age. It was as if a veil had been torn from my eyes. Salvation was preached to me, and all I knew was I didn't want to go to hell. That thought kept me in line. I just wanted to please God, and because I didn't have any reason to question what I was taught, I easily became indoctrinated.

Change happened so fast, around me and inside me. Our mom introduced us to a friend she'd known growing up. Her name was Karen, and soon, she was with us more often than not. It was like Miss Keera all over again, except Karen had visible tattoos and piercings and was a lot edgier than Miss Keera. We didn't know it at the time, but Karen and Mom had a romantic relationship as well. But this go-round was a lot different.

Things started off well and quickly took a turn for the worse. Karen eventually moved into the house with us, and she brought with her a change I'll never forget. When my mother was around, Karen played the role of the nice guy, but as soon as Mom left, Karen treated my siblings and I like crap. It was as if she was trying to cause a divide in our family. When we spent time with Nee-Naw, we explained to her what Karen was doing and that we felt like our mom was choosing Karen over us.

I became emotionally fragile during this time, and the year Karen lived with us seemed very dark. My sister and I gravitated to Nee-Naw, who became like our second mother. She knew everything going on in our household and had our back against our own mother. I grew to resent our mother for failing to protect us.

Karen's attempts to dominate us by antagonizing us started with Erica and then trickled down to me. As Jaelyn grew older, she became a victim as well. We'd hit our knees crying out to God, asking him to remove Karen from our lives and give our mother a change of heart. We prayed, but brighter days never seemed to come. There were days when Nee-Naw would pull in front of our house to drop us off and we'd sit in the car for hours, dreading going inside. Nee-Naw could feel our pain and sometimes cried with us.

As our relationship with Nee-Naw grew, Erica and I gained an understanding of our family dynamics. We eavesdropped on conversations between Nee-Naw and Mom, and Nee-Naw often expressed her disdain for the relationship between Karen and our mom. It was never a negative conversation, but as children, we put the pieces together in our own minds. Our mother was in a romantic relationship with Karen

This chasm created between my mother and me happened over time, like a slow-acting but lethal injection of rejection and hurt. My mother grew angry and bitter.

She became unforgiving and unapologetic, and to me, she was no longer the same mom I'd had when we lived on Fairdale Street. I couldn't wrap my mind around not being number one to my mom anymore. It cut deep, and still, the scars remain. In my early childhood, I'd been the biggest mama's boy on earth, but I was being forced into a hole, sinking further and further away from the love I once knew.

There was a major shift in our household, and my insecurity and self-doubt grew. Where we were once raised on love, now all my sisters and I could think about was survival. It took a toll on us. Our only outlet and the only person who understood was Nee-Naw, and she often came to our defense and rescued us. Church with Nee-Naw became our safe haven, the only place we could run to for love and support. I could no longer look to my mom for comfort and peace as my refuge. Our house wasn't a home anymore. Instead, it felt like my personal hell.

As I watched the verbal abuse between mom and Erica, I didn't know where to place my sympathy and allegiance. I was torn. I loved my mom deeply but couldn't understand why our family had changed so much. The pain we felt inside had to be put on the back burner because, not only were we emotionally scarred, but Mom also became physically abusive as she struggled to raise four kids.

Karen frequently deceived my mom into believing my sisters and I had done something wrong, and I started to feel as if I had to perform for my mother's love. Often, we were punished for no apparent reason. Even when there was a reason, the punishment didn't fit the offense. We were beaten and verbally mistreated, and most times, I believed Karen was behind it all. It felt like she was taking our mother from us. Our family had been in a downward spiral since Karen showed up. Nothing was the same. I questioned God every day as to why things had changed for us in such horrible ways.

Our living conditions were better than they had been in our old house, but my emotional state was a wreck. I felt as if my mom wasn't my mom anymore. She was just the dictator in our household, someone who waited for us to do wrong so she could punish us. And punishments became progressively worse. I watched Mom pull Erica up the stairs by her braids. At one point, I was made to kneel on rice. Good days were few and far between, and we walked on eggshells to try and give our mother peace and make sure she was taken care of for the sake of our own well-being. My sisters and I would ask each other what kind of mood Mom was in so we knew how to interact with her. If she was in a bad mood, our own anxiety and fear skyrocketed, but if she was in a good mood, we tried to keep it that way. It was hard because her mood could change very quickly.

Karen and Mom eventually split up after being together for years, but their relationship had turned our family upside down. As a result, my anxiety had grown astronomically, and I'd come to see love as something to be earned by performance. I was supposed to get good grades, clean the house well, and give my mom the right gifts for holidays and birthdays. I could only get my mother's affection, I believed, if I performed exactly how she wanted. I'd spend years striving to do well just to feel good enough in her sight. From this, I was broken and left in shambles.

Every day was a day of pain, but when it was bad, it was really bad. I saw sides of my mother I never thought were there, and she sometimes treated us as if we weren't her kids. This hurt me deeply and caused severe emotional trauma I carried for years. I no longer knew what unconditional love felt like. As I reached a critical time in my life, when I'd be starting middle school, I needed reassurance and strength. I was fighting demons and internal battles of my own and felt hopeless because my main lifeline had been demolished. I was dealing with an all-time-high identity crisis. Hell, at times I even looked for identity within Karen because she was the closest thing to a male role model I knew.

There I was, the only boy in a household full of women, lost, not knowing up from down. Craving understanding, craving a father. Looking for someone who could just get me. I desperately wanted to be heard, but my mom constantly shut me down because, as she said, explaining how I felt was "disrespectful." I eventually fell out of love with my mom. We'd have isolated moments of happiness within the household, but all joy was a distant memory. This wasn't the love I once knew. My heart grew heavy as I searched for answers, searched for hope, searched for a father. I just wanted someone to have my back.

Evolve Your Self with Emotional Intelligence

In a video for The School of Life, philosopher Alain de Botton says, "Emotional intelligence is the quality that enables us to confront with patience, insight, and imagination the many problems that we face in our affective relationship with ourselves and with other people." As a young child, I was taught empathy and to be very considerate of other people's feelings. At the same time, I struggled to navigate a lot of the emotions that came up in me as I experienced different situations. It was absolutely imperative for me, as I became an adult, to sort through and navigate my emotions with a certain level of intelligence to discern exactly what was going on. Had I not done this, I could either have become very hardened to a lot of sensitive situations, or I could have become completely broken and unable to piece myself back together.

Sorting through my emotions required a season of spending time by myself and getting to know me. I had to get very comfortable with being uncomfortable with the emotions I was experiencing and realize that it was okay to feel them. As a child, one of the things I wanted most was to hear from my mother that it was okay to feel exactly what I was feeling. When that failed me, I gave my identity and validation to the church. Not God, but the church. Because of church culture, I had to mask a lot of my deepest, most sincere feelings. Too often, my thoughts and emotions were frowned upon and considered sinful.

To be greatly successful in life requires the ability to intelligently navigate your emotions and the emotions of others. Without being intentional about the time you spend getting to know yourself and your feelings, you become susceptible to succumbing to the prison of other people's thoughts. Get to know you. Self-care, self-love, and self-appreciation are essential. Be true to your feelings and accept whatever consequences may come with them, and learn how to deal with other people's emotions with empathy and a desire to understand.

CHAPTER 4

Dad Who?

Any word of encouragement or advice was life-giving to this fatherless child. I wanted someone, anyone, to step up and treat me as a son. I didn't know sonship, and it became hard for me to respect authority because that void in my heart was often filled with defensiveness and anger. I felt unlovable. I dreamt of walking around the house in my father's shoes that were obviously too big for me, striving to be just like him. That was my light at the end of the tunnel, but the more I chased it the farther away from me it withdrew. Any manly advice would've been golden to me.

The pain gave birth to a new desire. I would find purpose, identity and peace to calm the emotional unrest. My calling in life was found in my church. The church experience for me was always oddly intriguing. The perfume from the old "mothers" hit my nose as I walked through the double doors and entered into the sanctuary. Each song drew an emotional response from everyone in the congregation. The music was loud and the preacher was louder. Church became a regular part of our weekly routine. Erica's alarm clock would go off, and her footsteps would grow closer to my door. "Jordan, wake up. Time for church," she'd say.

I soon learned that this church had been pastored by my great-grandfather, who was Nee-Naw's dad. So my grandmother, as the eldest of her siblings and the only one who still attended the church, was revered by the leadership and the congregation. That same respect trickled down to my sister and me since the rest of the church knew of our bloodline. I always felt a sense of pride as I walked through the doors of that church on the East Side of San Antonio.

My great-grandfather had been a prestigious preacher in the Pentecostal Assemblies of the World. Late in his life, he moved from Grand Rapids, Michigan, to take over as pastor of Faith Temple Apostolic Church, in San Antonio, which became the beacon of hope for many drug addicts, homeless people, sick people, and even some celebrities. David Robinson, who played center for the San Antonio Spurs and was a 10-time NBA All-Star, the 1995 NBA MVP, and a two-time NBA

Champion, was baptized by my grandfather, Horace M. Young, at that church.

Genuine love resonated throughout the church even after my great-grandfather's death in 1996. That same love kept me wanting more. The church became my extended family and friends. The people there respected me, and I finally had a sense of meaning and purpose to my life. I also discovered my life was larger than me. I was here on this earth to positively impact lives. Close friends of the family, my great-aunts and great-uncles, and especially my grandmother often told me I was next up to be a preacher, that I would follow in the footsteps of my grandfather.

At first, their predictions for my future felt like such an honor. But I didn't know Paw-Paw. I was only one year old when he died, but I was impressed by how highly people spoke of him. This calling never seemed intimidating. Instead, it seemed like my destiny and birthright, and I embraced it. Even as a small child, I was passionate about helping people and leading them to something greater. Another side of who I was had been awakened.

At that time, my mom had a stack of old VHS tapes of Paw-Paw preaching, and I watched them all. His preaching style gave me chills. He preached with so much conviction, and he captivated the hearts and mind of the people. He was very direct and never cut corners when telling the truth. Enthralled, I studied the videos, wanting to absorb every word. This was my calling in life. I was called to preach.

Nurturing and watering my calling, Nee-Naw tried her best to answer every question I had about our faith. "Nee-Naw, if God loves us, why does he allow bad things to happen to us?" I once asked. She gently explained, "What we perceive as bad, God orders to work in our favor. Always remember that, baby."

With this new sense of purpose and significance, I never wanted to leave my church. This was my new home. I made the decision to give my life to God, and the people of Faith Temple Apostolic Church became my new family. I served in the youth ministry, played the drums, taught classes, and even preached some sermons. I was at church Sunday mornings and Sunday evenings and for Tuesday night prayer, Wednesday night Bible study, Thursday night choir rehearsal, and Friday night family fellowships. I gave my all to serve God and to serve people and my identity was being shaped.

* * *

I turned to God and began to allow him to father me. My biological father was alive but never came around.

As a matter of fact, Jaelyn and I shared the same father, and it was important to my mom that we spend time at his mother's house to get acquainted with family members from his side. I grew very close with his mother and his sisters. They didn't live in a particularly nice side of town, but whenever we visited, we always had a good time. Being with them took me to a time and place different from what I knew because my grandparents grew up in the country, and even though they lived in the hood, they still had a country lifestyle. We spent countless days on the porch or hanging out in the garage, eating good food, singing songs, listening to good music, and playing cards or dominoes while the adults drank moonshine. I loved it.

Grandma ensured that we always felt her love despite the fact that my father was never around. Each time we visited her, I expected to see him, and I was always disappointed. Though, as far as I could tell, it didn't affect Jaelyn as much as it affected me. I believed my grandmother did so much for us not simply because she loved us but also to overcompensate for the void of our father not being there. My dad was a hustler and often ran the streets. Sometimes, he'd stop by Grandma's house to shower, get dressed, and leave within thirty minutes.

To this day, I've never had an in-depth, one-on-one conversation with my father. I don't know the man.

From an early age, his absence has hurt me to my core because I've always wanted to know who I was and thought I could find that in him. One day, my mom picked me up from Grandma's house and was curious as to why my head hung low. Inside, I was hurting. I was devastated that my dad didn't want to spend time with me. I felt like something was wrong with me. Like I was the ugly duckling or black sheep in his eyes. Looking back, I see it was never about me because I was just one of the seven children my father failed to take care of, but as a child I blamed myself.

My mother became irate and yelled at me when I explained I wanted my father in my life. It was misplaced anger that should have been reserved for my dad for being an irresponsible man. She questioned me about why I wanted to spend time with him and explained that I didn't need him. I quickly stopped crying and held back my tears. His absence and the absence of her understanding were two more scars added to my soul. The gaping void I felt in my heart only grew wider and deeper.

I was the only boy my mother gave birth to and the youngest boy my father brought into this world, and I felt as if no one really understood the pain deep in my heart. I watched as other fathers participated in their sons lives through academics or athletics. Fathers of close friends would come around and joke with my friends and I. They knew us and enjoyed our company. But not my father. I couldn't even tell you where he lived, and we lived in the same city.

I couldn't run to my sisters because, though they knew my situation, they really couldn't empathize with what I was feeling. I couldn't run to my mother to explain the situation because her frustration would be misplaced and taken out on me, and I didn't want to cause any friction between us. So I dealt with it by myself. To cope, I grew hard and cold. I never wanted anyone to be able to make me feel like that again. If I was going to do bad, I could do bad all by myself.

All I ever wanted was to hear that man tell me he was proud of me, that I was enough. I didn't want validation from anybody other than the man who gave me my last name. I wanted to feel like somebody. I wanted to be somebody. I wanted to have my own identity because, ultimately, I loved my father and would have given anything and everything just to have him in my life. But he wasn't there.

The reality was he couldn't be there. The one thing that prevents a man from being a good father is that he isn't finished being a little boy. It was no excuse, but it comforted me through the agony I experienced. As his child, I was left with a hole in my soul that only my dad could fill—and he chose not to fil it. Ultimately, my journey wouldn't be one of learning to forgive him. It would be to forgive myself for believing there was something lacking within me that caused his absence.

Evolve Your Self
with Identity

A lack of identity greatly affected me because, as a child, I never had that key example as to what and who I was to become. I spent many years feeling this void of not knowing who I was, and it crushed me. I looked for my identity wherever I could find it. One day, my sister's boyfriend, who we knew from church, came over to pick her up, and I ran upstairs and put on clothes to dress exactly like him. He was a teacher like I wanted to be. He was a drummer like I aspired to be, and he was an athlete like I desired to be. He became one of the greatest influences in my life for a time. I ran downstairs ready to go out the door, with him and my sister, and everyone laughed at me because I was dressed exactly like him. He had become my source of identity.

My mother asked, jokingly, "Jordan who are you?"

I cried and shouted, "I don't know who I am." For the first eight years of my life, I had seen no model for who

I was to become. I wrestled with this for a while, but when my grandmother introduced my sister and I to church and to God, that became my identity. For a time, the church nurtured my gifts and the things I liked to do in my life. It watered my heart and gave life to a lot of the abilities I didn't know I had. And so my identity was wrapped up in the image of Christianity.

The Hebrew word for Father is Abba, and Abba means source. Since I didn't have a father in my life, my identity was hidden from me. But I'm not alone in that. We live in a day and time when majority of the world is at an all-time high identity crisis. So many of us don't know who we are, so we become somebody else, living somebody else's dream, looking and sounding just like another person, mimicking athletes, artists, and social influencers.

But the question that was posed to me at eight years old still remains the same at twenty-five. Who are you? What is your source? What gives you your identity?

Nobody can answer these questions for you, but if you desire to achieve greatness, you must answer them. Finding your identity in life is hard, but necessary. When you don't know who you are, you'll inevitably try to become someone else, living out someone else's dreams, goals, and thoughts for your life. Greatness can't be achieved in your life without fulfilling your unique destiny.

It doesn't pay to imitate anyone else. Imitations are cheap. When you become who you are, you don't waste time becoming someone else. Sadly, most people die as someone else.

Write out twenty words or phrases that describe who you are—the good, the bad and the ugly. Next, write out twenty things that describe how others may view you. Last, ask yourself if those things are true and whether or not they align with who you think you are. The power is not in "finding" yourself but becoming yourself, flaws and all, and loving who you turn out to be.

CHAPTER 5

Stop Crying

Soft and weak-kneed, I constantly felt sorry for myself. There were qualities I needed to possess in order to evolve into the man I needed to be. Had someone not come along to water that seed in my life, the outcome for me would be much different. None of the success I've acquired would've been possible without this attitude adjustment. Coddling myself in the times of adversity, I expected the world to stop and pamper me. But I was quickly waking up to the harsh reality.

Meeting Brandon changed my life, vision, and perspective. Brandon is my uncle through marriage. He hasn't always been around, but I wish he had been. Brandon was my cousin's, stepfather. Quincey, my cousin, was my ace, my best friend, and brudda. We did everything together. I was always at his house, getting into trouble or just hanging out. Since he was older than I, I clung to him, letting him show me the ropes through what interested us both, sports.

Quincey simply had God-given athletic talent. It didn't matter how hard you worked, either you had it or you didn't, and Q had it. He wasn't the fastest or the strongest, but he had a unique ability to perform at the highest level as an athlete and I wanted to be just like him. When Brandon became Quincey's stepfather, I finally got a male figure to guide me through my mental chaos. His presence gave me a breath of life. He taught me critical lessons every person, man or woman, needs to heed. He taught me one principle in particular that I would come to live by and which would make all the difference in everything I did as I grew.

While I was there one day, Quincey decided we would go into the back yard to train. That summer, we were conditioning our bodies for the following season, when I'd be joining him at our high school. Uncle Brandon had a lot of sports and training equipment around the house, so Quincey and I took advantage of it. We put on helmets and shoulder pads to perform drills. While we were running drills, Uncle Brandon made his way to the back yard and took over our training.

Uncle Brandon had us run Oklahoma drills, a one-on-one hitting drill where one person has the football and the other tackles him. But there was one problem.

I was a runt. My cousin was more skilled than I was, he was much bigger, and outweighed me by at least fifty pounds. I was terrified to go against Quincey, and my fear was evident in the timid way I ran at him. I felt like David up against Goliath, but without a slingshot. Quincey knew the eyes of his stepfather, were on him, and he had to turn the heat up. What started out as just a fun time turned into a nightmare of competition.

Quincey wasn't the type to take it easy on me either. He relished throwing me to the ground to "make me better." He knew I was incapable of challenging him in any way, and after several attempts at tackling him and getting clobbered so my face met the dirt, tears of disappointment poured down my face. I felt sorry for myself, and I searched for sympathy, but I found none.

All of a sudden, I was face to face with Uncle Brandon, who screamed at me a lesson I'll remember for the rest of my life. "Don't ever come back out here going through these drills half-ass," he said. 'Whatever you do in life, make sure you're the best at it. Don't do anything, whether it be football, joining the band, or playing the drums at church, halfway. Be the best at it, or don't do it at all!"

When I thought he was going to show me compassion, he gave me something much more valuable, and the lesson stuck. He taught me how to fish for life and feed my family forever. I've harnessed this mentality to attack every dream, every goal, and all of my ambitions. I'm not fighting to outdo the person to the left or to the right of me but simply to become the best version of myself every single day. I can't be satisfied with patting myself on the back for what I did today because I know tomorrow will require me to step up my game. Thanks to Uncle Brandon, I learned to thoroughly love and enjoy the process and pursuit of becoming the best at whatever I set my mind to doing.

No one had ever spoken to me that way before, especially when I was clearly upset. My mom would have babied me, but Uncle Brandon told me what I needed to hear. It was the first time a grown man gave me a life lesson that wasn't about sports or spirituality. It was a key to success in life. No one cares about those tears!

Evolve Your Self with Emotional Intelligence

Your mindset will determine your overall outcome for your life. Going through the various trials and tribulations I went through spiritually, emotionally, and physically, I could have easily gotten stuck. Instead, I had to grab ahold of the reins of my mind to change my life.

Growing up in church, I learned from the Bible that one of the key skills God encourages us to acquire is understanding. My pastor once complimented me by saying I have a unique ability to understand. Understanding can make a difference in every life situation. You may not be able to change the given circumstances around you, but you can control your mindset—your thoughts, beliefs, and how you choose to see those circumstances.

I constantly try to gain detailed understanding so that my mind isn't worn down or pressed with anxiety.

The difference between a six-figure or seven-figure earner and a minimum-wage employee is simply mind-set. I had to start thinking about myself in my situations a lot differently.

A lot of people exercise their bodies and strive to make more money in life, but the ultimate adjustment you need to make in order to succeed in any area of your life is an adjustment of the mind. Think about what you think about. Question the thoughts and beliefs that keep you stuck and choose to replace them with thoughts that will help you move forward in life.

CHAPTER 6

When in Doubt, Bet on Yourself

Graduating high school was like a lifetime achievement award in my household. It was one of those accomplishments that was expected of you but was still held in high regard. No one in my immediate family was a college graduate, so getting your high school diploma was an honor. Strutting like I ain't never walked before, I floated across the stage, listening to the roar of celebration I received from my classmates and family. While I basked in the glory of simply walking the stage and grabbing my diploma, most of my friends' worried over whether they were graduating with honors or not.

For years, my academic self-worth had been low. I'd never fit the mold of how my teachers wanted students to learn, and few teachers had made the effort to teach me in the ways I learned best. My lack of achievement had convinced me I was average, and somewhere along the way, I started doing just enough to get by and stay on the football team. I came to believe my low scores exposed a lack of intelligence in me, so when I actually graduated, I relished in the moment.

Most of the friends I played football with were going on to four-year universities on full-ride scholarships to play football and pursue their education. Although I was excited for them, I couldn't help hanging my head because, as much as I wanted to, I wouldn't get to follow that path. As a high school student, I had no idea what an SAT or ACT was. I didn't know how to prepare for them or why I would even need to take them. The thought of asking my counselors for my transcript was comical because I knew the grade point average would reflect my lack of interest in academics over the previous four years.

The public school system had failed me. My teachers were incapable of honing and developing the true passions and desires I had. They couldn't measure my intelligence nor could they assist me in becoming who I wanted to be. They were just there to help me pass a test, not to help me blossom as a human. School had become not much more than a big social event to me. I was the popular nobody, infamous for my big mouth.

I had applied to a variety of colleges, but all I got in return were fancy letters stating "You do not meet the requirements . . . blah, blah, blah." If I was honest, that wasn't the life I wanted for myself anyway. That was my mother's fantasy. She wanted the best for me, but college wasn't it. I had to search within to find what was truly going to give me fulfillment, a hard decision to make for a seventeen-year-old kid. There wasn't a blueprint for the path I'd eventually embark on. I was going to have to be innovative and blaze my own way.

* * *

That summer after graduation, it quickly became clear that I needed more than just a high school diploma to create the life I wanted for myself. Truthfully, I had no clue what that looked like, but after listening to the wise counsel of a barber from my city, who put the first pair of clippers in my hands, I decided I didn't want to work for anyone. I would pursue self-employment. Becoming a professional barber was the route I chose, but this came at a cost. It made me feel inadequate next to my peers. Not only that, I also felt the pressure to become a first-generation success story.

At the time, I wasn't as passionate about barbering as I was about creating my own business. I was taking a chance on myself and honing the skills to become a successful barber. I had to find within myself the wherewithal to silence the external noise of other people's opinions. Even the chatter of my own family. But even after this victory, I was quickly met with another opposition.

Unfortunately, I didn't have the funds to pay the tuition for barber college. I could've allowed this challenge to slow me down but my determination to make something of myself and not fall behind was too great. To get out the house while my mom went to work, I spent time at the local barber shop with some friends who graduated before me. They were barbers, and they suggested I apply for a scholarship program for barber college. Mom and I jumped on her laptop and applied for the program. Luckily, I received a small scholarship, enough to cover my deposit for barber college.

However, the new class for barber college wouldn't start until October. So I spent months in my thoughts, coming up with creative ways to attract clientele. Once the school year started again, Mom, Jaelyn, and Amayah all took off for work or school each morning, and I was left waiting for what seemed like an eternity for something to break through for me. Most days, as I sat around the house, I tried to promote my barbering business through Facebook or Instagram, while only cutting a head or two ever week. Most days I spent lounging around house. I'd sit on my mom's bed and watch movie after movie on BET.

One day, a commercial came on for ICDC, a for-profit college promoted by Lil' Romeo and Master P. I jotted down the number and made the phone call. Exercising patience had never been my talent as I anxiously craved some progress. I wanted to feel accomplished, and this path seemed as good as any. I called the number and spoke to a counselor about tuition and other fees for enrollment in the school. I was determined to make it happen, but I had no idea what I was doing. That dream lasted a day before it was out of sight and out of mind. The very next day, as I repeated my daily routine, a commercial for an aeronautics school in Oklahoma ran, and I jotted down that information. Becoming an airplane engineer wouldn't be so bad, I thought. That idea quickly faded too.

At eighteen years old, I was trying to figure out my life, and I was grasping at whatever opportunities came up in the moment. It was like I'd awakened in this thing called adulthood, and somehow, I was supposed to go from raising my hand in a classroom for permission to use the restroom to having a step-by-step plan of what my life should look like as an adult. I didn't have a guide, so I'd have to figure it out on my own.

I figured barbering was the final resort for me, and I was determined to make this my career because I had no plan B. I wasn't an incredible barber, far from it, but I was really good at selling myself and making people believe I was the best barber for them. I was passionate about turning what started as a dream into a reality. This wasn't just a hobby for me. It was going to be the conduit I'd use to get me out of my family's devastating financial crisis.

October finally rolled around, and it was time for me to begin barber college. Money in our household was at an all-time low, as my mother settled for working dead-end jobs, including a position as a special education teacher's assistant at the school across the street from our neighborhood. The job paid almost nothing but it was paycheck. My mother sacrificed so I could use her car to get to and from school. In the scorching South Texas heat or the harsh winter, she walked home just so I could pursue my career. This was a significant sacrifice as she had three other children, two of whom were still living in her household, and she had to provide for them on her own.

Embarrassment and shame plagued my thoughts as I drove to barber school each day, knowing my mother would have to walk in whatever conditions Mother Nature dealt her. As the only boy in a single-parent household, I felt the responsibility to provide for my mother and siblings and make life easier for them. I was torn between staying back or finding rides each day and using my mother's vehicle to get to school. Most times, I felt frustrated. It wasn't my fault that we were struggling. I wondered why my path to success had so much friction. I didn't understand why my mom was struggling and why I had to endure this frustration. I wondered why she couldn't just buy me a car the way my friends' parents had for them. She told me, "Jordan, if I had more, I would do more." But she had struggled to recover from a couple of layoffs and hadn't been able to get back on her feet the way she wanted. She would have given me anything, but she just didn't have it to give.

At the time, all I could see was that it was my turn to live. I believed I shouldn't have to suffer the consequences of bad decisions she's made in her life. I couldn't see that she was doing the best she could with the circumstances she'd been given. Before I started barber college, I made a commitment to complete every hour of the 1,500 hours required by the state no matter what, but I wondered if that made me a bad son. Was I supposed to bear the weight of what she couldn't carry? Maybe, I thought, I should have been doing more to help her provide, but certainly God wanted me to pursue my own life's path.

I realized that where I was in life was not where I would always be. I decided to believe that God wanted the absolute best for me and came to the conclusion that it was time to take responsibility for my own life. Even though I didn't see many success stories around me, I stood solid on what my heart told me I could create from pursuing my passions in life.

I had a few friends from high school who had already completed their education at the same barber college I attended, and they shared insight as to who and what to watch out for. At orientation, the smells of Barbicide and hair products floated in the air. The aroma was all too familiar because it was the smell of the barber shop I'd gone to as a kid. As each person passed by, I was confused as to why some had on black smocks and others had on red smocks. I later found out the smock colors differentiated the beginners from the advanced students, who had been promoted to accept clients and could use their tools to cut hair on the floor.

Day one of barber college was like going to my first day of school all over again. The night before, I laid out my black pants, black shirt, and black smock, along with my black shoes—all the attire for barber college. Orientation had given me the chance to befriend some familiar faces, but I was still awkward and shy starting out. Still, despite what was going on at home, I was ready for my life to begin. Motivational speaker Eric Thomas said, "When you want to succeed as bad as you want to breathe, then you'll be successful." And I wanted it that badly.

Before we could pick up a pair of clippers and start taking clients on the barber school floor, we needed at least five hundred hours of book work and sanitation training. Our knowledge was measured by short tests we took at the end of each chapter. My instructor wasn't so good at the book work, so he'd just give us the answers to each test. Lucky for me. I wasn't good at test-taking anyway. I was there to cut hair and make money, period, not learn the long history of barbering, although some of the content was fascinating. I was surprised to learn barbers were the first doctors and dentist, and early barbers specialized in blood-letting and teeth extractions.

I wanted to graduate barber college so badly because my identity was tied to whatever success I could create. It was something I wanted to use to cover the insecurities I carried deep within me. As a self-employed barber, I would control my own ability to achieve, and I was amped to give that to myself instead of becoming an employee and depending on someone else to elevate my career.

Tips for Tuition

At the time I enrolled in barber college, I was also working at the Boys and Girls Club, and I figured the income
I received from the job would pay the balance of my
tuition. I attended barber college from eight in the
morning until two o'clock in the afternoon, and I had
to be at work by three o'clock. I drove an hour from my
home to barber college and then almost another hour
back in the opposite direction of school to go to work.
When I woke up each morning at six o'clock, I immediately clicked my YouTube app to play videos of Eric
Thomas and Les Brown, which supplied me with the
motivation and inspiration I needed.

Les Brown, whose work my mom had introduced to
me, taught me how to endure the hardships life would
bring and to persevere in spite of them. From Les

Brown, I found Eric Thomas, who taught me to take ownership and responsibility for the things I wanted to bring to fruition in my life. These men became my mentors, my teachers, and ultimately the voice of reason when it came to my entrepreneurial journey. They helped shape in me the mindset necessary to be successful. They gave me the blueprint for how anyone who has ever been successful had to think. There were many lessons I hadn't learned growing up in my childhood home that these two men provided me. They gave proper perspective on what my outlook should be given where I was in my life.

Getting ready each morning, I inevitably felt anxiety because I had a responsibility to make something of myself. Knowing the sacrifices my mother was making, I had to be great, and clocking into the Boys and Girls Club each day, I was frustrated. I didn't want a nine-to-five. I couldn't stand the idea of having a boss, having someone lord over me each day as I performed my job. I wanted to be the boss. I wanted to control my time, energy, and ultimately, my own destiny. There was so much more potential for what I could achieve in the barbering industry, working for myself. Working twenty hours a week for nine dollars an hour wasn't it. Still, each pay day excited me because I had no other consistent income.

I'd only been working at the club four months when I made the decision to quit. I'd had enough. My boss, Colleen, a redhead in her mid-thirties, constantly tried to show her superiority over me. She'd been working with the organization for years, but she micromanaged my every move and always had an opinion to share about what I was doing wrong. I was never allowed to just do my job. I needed out, so I made the decision to part ways with that job and go full-time in barber college.

There I was, stepping out on faith and completely trusting my grind and hustle to support my dreams and goals. With no money saved up, no car of my own, no loans, I decided it was time. I became a full-time student at barber college and spent fourteen hours a day there. From sun up to sun down, I slaved on the barbershop floor, servicing clients and finishing book work and sanitation necessities, some days without even having lunch. I was committed to never working a nine-to-five ever again, and I quickly became known around the school as one of the most driven teenagers they'd ever seen. The tips I received from each client who sat in my chair became the money I used to pay off the rest of my tuition. I carried all of my cash in a bright-pink Nike backpack, and each month, I plopped it on the front counter to count out my payment to our advisor.

Jelani Johnson, a barber from the Southside of Chicago spoke life into me as a teenager, encouraging me and affirming the brilliance I possessed at such a young age. This gave me the confidence I needed to continue to learn and absorb as much knowledge as possible in barber college. It made me feel good to know someone of his skill appreciated what I brought to the table. It definitely motivated me further.

Evolve Your Self with Perseverance

The success I create in my life is no accident. Overcoming doesn't just happen. I don't just stumble across my blessings. There were many days and countless nights when I had no drive, effort, or passion to keep going, but perseverance pushed me onward. The ability to persevere required me to practice consistent positive self-talk and develop unwavering focus. I knew things wouldn't always be the way they were then—but only if I kept going.

When I first became a barber, it was imperative for me to match my work to the best work I'd seen. Back then, those experts completely trumped the quality of my work. To improve, I studied the work I wanted to mirror. I learned that, when I looked at my own canvas, as an artist does, I had to be able to see the end from the beginning.

THE EVOLUTION OF SELF

Perseverance is the hard work you do after you've already done hard work. I wasn't content with lowering myself back into mediocrity because it was a comfortable place to be. I wanted to rise higher, and that meant I had to develop a certain level of buoyancy to bounce back from every storm and dark area in my life. When you build the muscle of perseverance, it becomes easier to bounce back from any situation life hands you.

I developed the mindset that I wasn't content with playing the cards I was dealt. I decided to rip up the cards and create my own game. I focused on the prize and realized the suffering I was going through was nothing compared to the joy awaiting me.

If you're going to acquire any success in your life, perseverance is necessary. Your dreams and goals lie on the other side of your perseverance. Grab the legacy you'll leave by the reigns and endure the hardship of being too tired to get to the life and business you want to create.

CHAPTER 8

Tested

Barber college was supposed to last me all of nine and a half months, but because of a family vacation we took for Thanksgiving, I needed ten months to finish school, resulting in overage payments. For every hour over, I had to pay out of pocket, and I accumulated over $400 in overages. I had no idea how I could come up with that money. Luckily, because of my reputation as outgoing and hardworking during my time in school, the owners allowed me to finish the hours for free.

When all was said and done, I'd accomplished a major milestone in my life and I was on my way to what was then my ultimate goal, to become a licensed barber. I passed my written exam and last was my practical exam. It was time to put into action, in front of the state board, everything I'd been taught. One of the student instructors had taken his practical exam and failed. "He was one of the best," I thought. "If he failed, I certainly won't pass."

Butterflies filled my stomach as I walked towards the main entrance of the state board exam. I recognized a familiar face, one of the students from barber college, as we headed in. He was an older gentleman with gray hair. Seeing him there helped me calm down because I had someone there who received the same education I did, so if I found myself stuck or lost, I could watch him to get back on track.

I walked in and tried to fake a smile so the three women overseeing the exam might somehow show me favor and overlook some of my mistakes. I had never been so nervous in my life. If I failed this exam, I didn't know if I could retake it, and if so, how long I'd have to wait. Questions plagued my mind. I didn't want to be a screw-up. Most of all in that moment, I wanted to make my mother proud. I wanted her acceptance.

I carried a duffel bag full of all the equipment and tools I needed and made a beeline to my station. As I entered the exam room, I remembered from our practical exam training that sanitation was sixty to seventy percent of the test. I had to make sure my hands were constantly sanitized by washing them or using the hand sanitizer at my station. I patiently waited for the instructors to give us directions on what we should do next.

There were three barbers taking this exam. To the left of me was a guy who'd failed but was back to retake the test, and to the right of me was the older gentleman I knew from barber college. We were all nervous, and an eerie silence swept the room as we stood there, anticipating our instructions. We had to perform a haircut on a live model, demonstrate a fade on a live model, and then perform a shave on the model. That was all easy for me, but after that, we had to section the hair on a dolls head into three parts and perform a different technique on each section. It wasn't my specialty as a barber, and it was incredibly nerve-racking for me.

By the end of the exam, my lower back was drenched with sweat. I packed up everything, and I waited in the lobby for my results. The guy before me passed and made it known he had done so. Next, was the older man from barber college. I just knew he'd passed his exam. He'd paid attention to every detail and was the calmest throughout the test. But sadly, the look of disappointment on his face told me otherwise. He'd failed. With his head hung low in disappointment and disbelief, he walked back to his truck. I was next. I was in the grip of the most excruciating nervousness I'd experienced in my life.

Finally, the proctor called me back into the exam room. Snatching the paper from her hands and without saying thank you, I looked at my results. I had passed! I was an official barber in the state of Texas. Right away, I called a friend I'd gone to high school with who was opening a barbershop and had agreed to let me work there. We were both excited, and we were ready to get to work.

CHAPTER 9

Pain Is Your Provision

After finishing barber college, I began my journey as a barber and entrepreneur, but there was a lot of financial and emotional friction going on in my house. I wanted to live my own life, but I felt as if I bore the cross of my mother's problems. Her situation was holding me back.

A friend of mine, Ced, who was a few years ahead of me in high school and who graduated from the same barber college as I did, was opening his own barbershop in the countryside of San Antonio, in a small city called Selma. In high school, Ced and I had both played football, and I'd watched him cut hair in the locker room. He owned property in Selma, and on that property was a mobile home and a garage. This property was so old that it still had a well from which you could fetch water.

Since I didn't have a car, I figured it was the perfect set-up for me. I could live and work on the same property and start a successful career.

I'd grown up in church with my friend Jonathan, and we decided to room together at Ced's place. I felt bad leaving home because I still felt responsible for my mom and sisters, but my desire for success was greater than my need to stay. My mother was very frustrated, very angry, and very bitter when I told her I was leaving. It was like she couldn't believe I would make the decision to leave the house when I knew what struggles she was facing.

Around this time, my mother had resorted to sending my siblings and me to clinical research trials to make money to pay the mortgage. The process left me ashamed, and I wondered why God would allow it to happen to us. Why couldn't my family have inherited wealth? Why did we have to struggle? When was God going to turn our situation around? At what point were prayers going to stop being words spoken to a ceiling only to bounce right off and smack me in the face? It was easy to point the finger and try to place the blame somewhere. I blamed my father, my mom, myself, and hell, sometimes I even blamed God.

With so much stored-up ambition, animosity, and pressure to create something new, I left. It wasn't easy leaving my mom and my sisters behind because I was the oldest in the household. I was the voice of reason for my siblings. They looked up to me, they depended on me, and they loved me. But I was evolving, and it was time to spread my wings and fly.

My mother wanted me to completely clean the room from top to bottom before I left, and I just wanted to pack a few items and be on my way. In response to her demands, I threw all my high school memorabilia and my old clothes and shoes in the trash. This, of course, only made her angrier, as I carried things to Jonathan's car, my mother screamed at me, telling me I was trashing all of my memories from growing up there.

I argued back and forth with my mom, as I made my way down the stairs. Before it was over, she screamed, "Don't you ever come back to this house!" She spit sunflower seeds on me and threw whatever she could grab at me and finally poured a cup of juice on me as I made my way out the door. This was the straw that broke the camel's back. The chapter of having to succumb to the pain that came with living in my mother's household was closing. The constant fighting and the uneasy atmosphere she created were now behind me. I was done constantly feeling heavy, misunderstood, abused physically and emotionally.

I never wanted to live with my mother again. I never wanted my household to be the one I grew up in. I was determined to create something new. A place of peace and comfort where I could be expressive and creative and flourish. In my new home, what my mother had laughed at would be watered and developed by me. I never wanted to argue with her or anyone ever again.

I got into my friend Jonathan's car. He'd had a completely different ending to his time living in his parents' household, and the look on his face when he saw the juice on my white T-shirt was a puzzled one. It was an awkward and quiet car ride to Selma, but he didn't ask any questions. I felt free but crushed at the same time. I wished my mother could just be happy for me.

*   *   *

When we made it to Cedric's place, I took my things out of Jonathan's car and marched up the few stairs to the mobile home's front door and into the room I'd claimed when I scoped out the house to see if I wanted to live there. All I had to my name were clothes, a cell phone, and a phone charger. Johnathan, on the other hand, had it all—clothes, a car, jewelry, and a lot more money than I had. I saw everything he had as motivation to work hard to get what I wanted. I wouldn't carry myself as if I didn't have enough. I kept my head up, dressed well, and kept a smile on my face so the world wouldn't know the trauma I carried around inside.

Out of the closet, Cedric, pulled an old, urine-stained mattress for me to sleep on. Luckily, I'd grabbed sheets and my comforter from my bed, or I would have had some very cold nights. The house smelled like it had been there centuries, and everything had a dusty, vintage look. The blue carpets weren't very welcoming, and the old paint on the walls and matching border did little to create the feeling of home.

It was a bittersweet moment for me because it was a new beginning, but all the while, I felt so empty inside. With my life at home in shambles and no steady income from my career, all I could do was work hard. I ended up helping Cedric convert what was supposed to be a garage into a just-stable-enough barbershop. I had never laid tile before, but we had to get it done. My motivation was that this would be the very shop where I would create a booming business, but the white tile with black grout was a complete disaster. We spent so much time renovating this garage that it almost made me feel like I had ownership in the building. I believed in Ced's vision, but ultimately, I was driven by the one I had for myself.

I was proud of what we created, but I knew this was just the hard work that had to be done before even more hard work was applied. Once everything was up and running, I was ready to cut hair, to prove myself, to show my skills and how much I truly wanted to be successful. Cedric had told me that Jose, the barber he'd previously worked with in that garage, had left enough clients for me to make enough to at least pay the bills while I built my clientele. Jose had gone on another binge and was nowhere to be found. It was the perfect opportunity for me to take over a sustainable clientele. I figured I'd pick up where he left off, but that wasn't the case.

As the days went by, I noticed Cedric's chair had someone new in it almost every thirty minutes. My chair was empty, and I grew frustrated. I had the skills. I just needed the opportunity to prove myself. Cedric was branding and marketing himself, and I figured I could do the same, so I printed some flyers on his home printer and began to promote myself. I put the last of my money towards business cards.

With flyers in hand, Cedric and I developed a marketing strategy to bring more clients to our barber chairs. We had no license or permit to do so, but around midnight, we darted across the street into a pitch-black neighborhood to post our flyers inside residents' mailboxes. We didn't know if it was legal or not, but it was the plan. Desperate times called for desperate measures, and we were willing to risk it all, or at least I was.

I allowed a few days to go by to see if our marketing strategy had worked. Turned out, it failed. Cedric had been out of barber college years before I started and had already built enough clientele, so he was still okay. But I wasn't. The days went on, and there was no return on our investment. I felt deflated. I spent my time sitting in the house, twiddling my thumbs or playing with Cedric's red nose pit bull puppy, while Ced was cutting hair. I wondered how long things would be that way.

I felt like Clip, the dog, was the only one who understood me and sympathized with what I was going through. I told Clip my problems as if he could understand, but all he did was raise an ear and come over to lick my hand. Many nights, I went to sleep bawling my eyes out. I was seeing three or five clients a week, fellow church members who knew I was cutting hair, and occasionally a client or two Cedric threw my way. But I was too far away for most of the people who would have been my clients to come to me for cuts.

I often thought of a video clip I'd watched of Will Smith while at my mother's house. In the video he'd reflect on how he grew up and knew that where he was not where he'd always be. And that was the same way I felt. My ambition and my determination were the only hope I had. I was struggling financially, sinking deeper and deeper into an ocean of debt and bills. I was flat out broke, and without a car. Johnathan had a job and a car and was gone for majority of the day. He didn't come home until around ten o'clock at night, so I was alone most of the day.

I had no transportation or money to go buy myself simple things like body wash, food, or anything to entertain me. I waited until Johnathan and Cedric were asleep to take my shower each night. It was humiliating not to have any money for body wash, so I would sneak into the kitchen to use the Dawn dish soap to wash my body and my hair. While they slept, I'd sneak to the kitchen, digging through the cabinet to find food. One night, I opened a can of tuna fish with a knife and squeezed in mayo from the local Chick-fil-A just to put some nourishment in my body. I even got so desperate that I tried to eat the sardines that had been in the cabinet for God knows how long. I'd never had sardines before, and they were horrible.

With my home rent and booth rent and other bills adding up, I had to make a decision. I couldn't stay in that situation and create the lifestyle I wanted. Still owing Cedric $500 for rent, I made a phone call that changed everything. I called my mother and apologized for whatever hurt I'd caused her months ago. I told her I needed to move back home.

Biting my nails with the anxiety, worried she'd tell me no, I let out a sigh of relief when I heard her say yes. But she had one condition. In the past, I had cut hair and serviced my clients inside the house in her office space. I could no longer do so. I had to move all of my barbering equipment outside to the garage. This was right around Thanksgiving, so it was very cold in San Antonio Texas. Cutting in the garage with no ventilation was tough especially during the winter, but I had to make do.

Evolve Your Self with Dedication and Commitment

Becoming dedicated and committed to completing a specific task was a turning point in my life. This change required self-discipline. I had to take a step back in my life and see where I was dedicating my time, energy, and effort. I had to learn it's possible to be dedicated and committed to the wrong things. I had to focus on the areas that needed certain restrictions and discipline, like time. I couldn't participate in every party or gathering. I had to discipline myself and govern myself according to the new life I wanted for myself.

The difference between the person who makes it in life and the person who doesn't is simply one's ability to remain focused and dedicated to a task at hand. In today's society, so many people are busy, but being busy didn't serve me. Being busy was the greatest adversary to being productive. You can be dedicated and committed to work that keeps you busy, or you can be dedicated and committed to your specific dreams and goals in your life.

I dedicated and committed a year of my life to barbering. While I was in school, I didn't allow myself to be pulled in every direction. I buckled down and focused on the task at hand. In a world where everything is grabbing at your attention, the real challenge is to remain focused. In order to remain dedicated and committed to a task, you have to understand your why. Though I wanted to party, though I wanted to hang out, though I wanted to go to the movies, I had to remember that my why was greater than the short-term pleasure I was seeking. Finding your why is discovering what pains you, what makes you cry, what burdens your soul, what brings you joy, and what makes you feel you must react. There is a unique trait we must possess that allows our brain to run towards pain. Your growth will only come through this discomfort. Marry discomfort so that which was once uncomfortable becomes familiar, leading to your on personal success.

· CHAPTER 10 ·

There Is No Finish Line

Having no idea about the conditions I'd been living in, Mom came and picked me up. I was happy to just see her face, and I could tell brighter days were ahead. It felt so good to be in the comfort of home with her and my sisters. And I no longer had to struggle for the things I'd once taken for granted, like food. But I knew the move was temporary. I could let my hair down and relax a bit, but I still had goals to meet.

While I was living with Ced, he had asked me one day if I could open his garage to show another barbershop owner some chairs he had for sale. I was at home the entire time, so I had no problem doing him a favor. Sitting in the mobile home and waiting for clients to hit me up, I was playing with Clip when I got the text message: "The guy is on his way."

A black truck pulled in front of the garage, and a man got out. As I showed him the barber chairs Cedric had for sale, the barbershop owner asked me what my name was. I replied "Jordan McCook," and I could see wheels turning in his head. "That name sounds familiar," he replied. "I believe I heard your name in the shop I own before."

I felt proud and happy that at least somebody was talking about me while I was miles away. He asked "Do you know Charlie, Dwight, or Luz?" I said, "Of course. Those are friends of mine from barber college." The conversation felt like a reply to my SOS (Save Our Ship). My friends had mentioned my name as a barber who could potentially work in the shop with them. Ron Dixon offered me his business card and told me, if I ever wanted to move and join the team at King's Mane Barbering, his door was open. In that moment, I had declined because I believed in what I was building with Cedric.

After I made the decision to move back in with my mother that November, I had to play chess instead of checkers. I had to move more strategically or else my life wouldn't play out the way I wanted it to. I began to take ownership and responsibility for every decision I made about my career and my life. I did what I had to do and set up a corner in my mother's garage that became my barber station where I serviced my clients. With the little money I had, I bought space heaters for the cold months ahead. I got creative with my marketing. As I sat around my mother's house by myself, while my younger sisters were at school and my mother was at work, I developed my Facebook and Instagram skills to promote my barbering business.

More church members became clients, and a couple of my friends, whose hair I'd cut in high school, were still faithful and came to me. Unfortunately, the barber college I went to was almost an hour away on the opposite side of San Antonio, and I had developed a clientele on that side of town that wasn't translating back to the northeast side where I lived. Working in my favor was that I was back where I was raised and had a lot of high school friends nearby.

As I tried to navigate my entrepreneurial journey, my relationship with my mother was still unstable, but I was dependent on her. I kept my head low and did what I had to do around the house for my sisters and for my mother. I made sure the house was clean and things stayed in order so there would be no friction between her and me.

After multiple unanswered calls to Ron, he finally responded and I was ecstatic. He wanted to interview me so he could learn a little bit more about my character and see if I really was a good fit for King's Mane. He invited me out to eat at a restaurant I'd never heard of before. Determined to get there, I borrowed my mother's car and arrived early. The interview felt natural because I spoke openly about what I wanted in a job and in my career. By the time we were done, the job was officially mine.

The next step was to visit the barbershop, so I met Ron at King's Mane one evening. Blue radiant light from the EyeVac machines bounced off the floor, illuminating the place. I'd never seen anything like the touchless vacuums that swept up the hair from the floor of the barbershop. At Ced's, we used the traditional broom and dust pan. I had no idea you could click a button and sweep the hair into a vacuum, I was in awe.

The entire barbershop was squeaky clean and had a distinct prestige feel. Vintage barber chairs, husky toolboxes to hold clippers, I was home. This was a dream come true. After receiving my key to the shop on a Monday, I couldn't wait for work to start on Tuesday. It was like the feeling of starting your first day of school, and I laid out my outfit the night before, excited to join the crew at nine o'clock the next morning. The barbershop offered "Great $10 Tuesdays" for walk-in clients, which was a perfect marketing strategy to create a large influx of clients and would be great for my first day.

Tuesday morning arrived, and I was ecstatic to start my new job. Dropping my mother off at work and going back home to get dressed for the day, it seemed like everything was working in my favor. Without the overwhelming bills I'd had in Selma, I decided to treat myself to a caramel macchiato from McDonald's to start my day. The smile couldn't be wiped off my face as I enjoyed the coffee drink. After cutting at Cedric's house and making $150 a month, finding a shop where I could make $150 to $200 in a day was a prayer come true.

The job was a great opportunity, but I failed to anticipate one problem. Some of the guys at the shop had tried to suppress my growth and my ambition when we were in barber college together. Because I was young and had no experience in life, they now tried to discredit me as a barber. But I wasn't going to allow anybody who had no vested interest in my success deter me from what I felt I deserved. Inevitably, I became the black sheep of the barbershop.

I was the youngest barber working amidst four veterans who had served our country and lived life twenty years before I was even born. In casual barbershop discussion, I was constantly told I didn't know anything and that my opinion wasn't valid because I hadn't lived long enough. This frustrated me because they knew nothing about me or what I'd been through in my life.

They had no idea who I was. I became isolated and focused on doing my job.

As I pulled away from that team spirit they tried to create in that barbershop, my coworkers looked at me funny. I didn't know how to operate as a part of a team in an industry that was so individualized. Operating as a team didn't register to me as growth for myself. I believed it was counterproductive to what I was trying to build.

One day, I came into the shop to get all the equipment and lights turned on before anyone else arrived. I was excited to start my day, but about thirty minutes after I'd set up and was waiting for clients, a short, stocky Army veteran coworker of mine, who later became the manager, came in, closed the curtains, locked the door, cut the TV off, and said he wanted to have a conversation with me. "Look," he told me, "I don't know who you think you are, but I'm going to tell you what is and what is not going to be in this barbershop. We work and operate as a team in here, so if you can't maneuver that way, then this may not be the barbershop for you. Your 'I don't care' attitude and arrogance aren't conducive for the overall atmosphere we're building in this barbershop. So if things don't change, you can leave."

I didn't see things that way. From my point of view, the problem wasn't that I had become arrogant but that I was no longer concerning myself with the opinions of my coworkers. I was there to focus on myself, to think for myself, and to produce for myself. I wasn't afraid to say I was the best barber in that barbershop. After being overlooked by so many clients because of my age, I had a chip on my shoulder. I had something to prove not just to the other barbers in the barbershop and not just to the clients who refused to sit in my chair, but to myself. I owed success to myself, and I was willing to do whatever it took to create success in my own life.

My response to him was short. "Okay," I told him, and we went back to business as usual. He had no authority to put me out of the barbershop. All he had was an opinion. But I listened and made adjustments going forward. I was going to be a team player and adhere to the team spirit. It was an attitude adjustment. I internalized the fact that these people weren't out to get me. They wanted to support me, but I shared the responsibility in supporting them as well. I stopped getting on the defensive when my coworker redirected me. I took it as an opportunity to grow. I began to get very comfortable with being uncomfortable, the underdog.

* * *

I'd approached my early days and, ultimately, the early months working in the barbershop with a chip on my shoulder because of the trials I was facing at home. The struggles and financial setbacks we faced every single day motivated me. I wanted to create something different for myself and my family, and that was all I could focus on. Going into my young adult years, my mother had instilled in me that I'd have to work for anything I was going to have in life, large or small. Nothing was going to be handed to me. That lesson was written on the tablet of my heart, so the desire to work and dedicate myself to excellence came naturally.

The first month working at the barbershop gave me mixed emotions. As the youngest barber, it was hard to gain the trust of clients and get them to sit in my chair, which meant I made minimal money. But my personality and big mouth compensated for the lack of money in my pocket. I became the life of the party, the jokester, the one who brought the entertainment and conversation to the barbershop. I didn't allow what I was facing at home to affect my drive and energy at work. I thoroughly enjoyed the barbershop because it reminded me of the conversation, attitude, and fun we had in the high school locker room.

No conversation was off limits. We openly discussed our views on politics, religion, sex, and life. Any conversation you shouldn't have in a corporate setting, we had. And I was there for it. It made going to work each and every day doable. During this time, my mother drove across the street from our neighborhood to her job every day. I would wake up a couple hours after her, get dressed, and then walk over to pick up the keys from her so I could go to work. I had no car of my own at the time. Everywhere I went, I had to ask for a ride. This was before Uber and Lyft rideshare services, so I was constantly phoning friends and coworkers to ask for a ride to and from work when my mother's car wasn't available.

Sometimes, I had to walk, but I felt as if God was allowing me to be in that situation so I could appreciate up. So many people can't appreciate up because they've never been down. What was going on in my life was just a paintbrush God was using to create this beautiful masterpiece of a success story he was making.

Within a couple of months, I was earning much more income than I'd ever earned in my life, and I began to talk to myself about my personal goals for work. I was dedicated and committed to becoming the best version of myself as a barber, entrepreneur, and overall hustler. My goal was to make at least $1000 a week. I would slide in the barbershop at sun-up and be there until sundown some days. On days when there were no clients walking in the shop, a coworker and I would go out in the winter of San Antonio and post our shop flyers to bring foot

traffic into our barbershop. I'm a firm believer in sow-
ing and reaping. The seeds I sowed in the cold days of
the year resulted in a harvest of clients in the weeks to
come.

As much as possible, I saved my money because I was
determined to have my own vehicle. After just a couple
of months, I'd saved up enough to have a conversation
with my mother about buying a car. I resented her at
the time because I thought she could've done a lot more
to help me. I tried to get her to cosign for a car loan, but
her credit wasn't sufficient. So I did what I've always
done and what I've always seen done. I made a way out
of no way.

I was desperate, ready to dive into a car loan of an
astronomical amount and bite the bullet for whatever
car note I had to make. Thank God I had support and
a voice of reason from my mother, who spent weeks
driving me around to different dealerships. After
many arguments between us—because like most kids,
I figured my mother had no idea what she was talking about—I finally came across a vehicle I liked on
Craigslist.

It was the last stop after a long day of car shop-
ping. We looked at the car on the website and figured
it was a good enough deal that we should check it out.
We went to the address the seller shared, and in May

of that same year, after just four months of working at King's Man, I purchased my very first car for $4000. On my own. No cosigner. No car payments. No financial assistance from anyone. What looked to everyone else like a Blue 2007 Pontiac G6 was to me a Lamborghini. Finally, I saw my efforts weren't going to waste. I saw that I literally can create whatever I wanted to create when I put in the hard work. Finally, I believed in the principles Mom had been trying to teach me through the car-buying process and all my life. And it was working in my favor.

I was in heaven. My car had a rainbow-sweet scent left behind by the young lady who'd previously owned it, and I inhaled deeply, grinning from ear to ear. As I drove home that night after making the purchase, I filled the car with loud music and screams of joy. I rode with the windows down, singing my favorite song. There was still a title switch to be done and insurance to buy, but I could finally say something was mine. I was so ecstatic. That same night I had to show it off, so I drove twenty minutes away to my sister's apartment just to show her and her friend, Rozlin. I wanted to show off my new car to the world.

In the following weeks and months, as I drove up and down each street in my neighborhood and the surrounding area, I remembered my days of walking and asking for rides from friends. I remembered all the friends who had cars in high school, long before I ever bought mine. I had to love, cherish, and appreciate what I'd earned for myself. Had I not gone through the process of struggling and budgeting to save enough money for my own vehicle, if I'd been handed a vehicle through no efforts of my own, I wouldn't have had the same appreciation for my car and the other belongings I have today. The process was necessary. Of course, with car ownership came a certain new sense of freedom, but since I was still living under my mother's roof, I still had to adhere to the rules of her household. Though I was nineteen years old, my mother raised us very traditionally. I had to abide by her curfew and constantly ask if I could go where I wanted to go. But I was gaining my own independence, manhood, and opinions on life. I felt, to a certain degree, that there was not much my mother could tell me because I was becoming the man I'd always wanted to be.

Because of the lack of money and the absence of a father figure, I always believed my mother wanted me to stay at home to contribute financially to her household. I questioned why I should have to suffer the consequences of her mistakes and put my life on hold to help her provide. Erica, my older sister had already moved out because of her constant fights with and disrespect towards my mother, so I bore the weight and responsibility of being the oldest in the house. I had two younger sisters to look after, and I had to help my mother around the house.

There were times when the mortgage, light bill, water bill, and other bills were due, and my mother attempted to get us to go to clinical research trials just to pay the bills. My younger sister, Jaelyn, who was four years younger than I, had already served as a lab rat to put a couple hundred dollars in my mother's pocket. Next was my turn. "Jordan I hate to ask this of you," my mother said, "but we need money for the mortgage. How do you feel about doing a clinical research trial for extra money?"

Hearing this shook me to my core. I had so many questions. Nothing inside me wanted to do this, but the pressure to be there in support of my family weighed on me. My mother painted the situation in a way that made me feel like, if I didn't do it, my family would end up living on the streets. The thought plagued my mind and caused a constant mental unrest. I hated being in this position and prayed better days would come. But the more I prayed to the heavens above the more it seemed like I'd never get the answers I wanted.

The research trial required me to stay three days in a facility without any outside contact. I had to be prepped and probed like a lab rat. I couldn't have my cell phone on my person at any time, and if I had to make a call, I was to use their phones. The whole experience was very scary and a very depressing time in my life.

I was conflicted. I wanted to live at home because I loved my mother and sisters, but at the same time, I didn't want this for my life. I couldn't stand the pressure of having to fulfill the role of a father as a teenager, and I carried that attitude around the house. I felt stifled in my growth and was often boisterous about it, and that wasn't going to fly with my mom. It was hard to voice my opinions as to how I should govern myself in my life when I was living in my mother's household and she believed she had the last say-so. I felt as if she wanted to reign lord over my life instead of allowing me to blossom and flow freely into who God was creating me to be. This conflict ultimately resulted in my mother kicking me out of her house.

I had nowhere to stay, so I called my sister, Erica, and her roommate, Rozlin, a close family friend, to see if they had room for me to live there. During this time, we were very involved in church, so my sister regularly opened her house for various youth events and singles fellowships. Because of this, friends from the church were always present, and it was like our own safe haven of friendship and fellowship. She opened her doors to me without question or concern. To move out of my mother's house and away from that situation into the light of my older sister's apartment was a dream come true.

At the time, Rozlin and her son, Manny, and my sister Erica and her daughter, Hailey, all lived in the two-bedroom apartment. But I was so excited to be out of my mother's house and finally have the liberty and freedom I'd always wanted, it didn't matter that both bedrooms were taken and I had to sleep on the floor. I could finally come and go as I pleased and didn't have to bear the burden of my mother's financial crisis.

* * *

Making $1000 a week with no car payment and only a cell phone payment and minimal rent to pay, I felt on top of the world. Nobody could tell me anything. I developed a certain level of cockiness and arrogance because I was finally financially stable. I wasn't even twenty years old, and I was making over $50,000 a year. I spent most of my time and money at malls and clothing stores. I purchased everything I'd ever wanted and went to the places I'd always wanted to see. I was making uncalled for purchases, like a $400 pair of cowboy boots from Cavender's that I only wore once or twice. I sent all of my clothes, including basic Hanes white T-shirts, to the cleaners. I was living without limits.

Around the city and in the barbershop community I became known as the loudmouth rookie. But my skills, barbering talents, and knowledge backed up my big mouth. I wasn't one of those young guys who had swag but no substance. I was knowledgeable beyond my years. Because I'd immersed myself in wisdom from my mentors, I understood certain laws of life that allowed me to stay ahead of my competition in the barbering industry. With all I was trying to achieve, I never drifted too far left or too far right because my biblical foundation held me true to my convictions. I wanted to please God, but at the same time, live like a rock star.

I was making more money than the vast majority of the people in my life. To someone who had only a short while earlier been nickel-and-diming and going to clinical research trials just to pay bills, $50,000 a year was a big number. I felt like I knew it all, and I carried that attitude when I spoke to people. I thought no one could stop what God had called me to do in my life. That all changed one night.

After a couple of months of living with my sister, I had settled in and gotten comfortable. I felt like it was my apartment, and I lost my attitude of appreciation. Each night, we all talked and caught up in the living room until we drifted off to our own sleeping quarters. Every night, I slept with a white, orange and yellow striped blanket even though I didn't own it. I'd grown accustomed to sleeping with this blanket, but one night, my sister decided that was the blanket she wanted.

This was Erica's apartment, and she had her own room for herself and my niece, but that night, she blasted her TV show in the living room while she curled up in that blanket. After bickering with her back and forth about who would use it, I walked over and snatched the blanket from her. Erica wasn't having it and demanded I give it back.

"Why don't you go lay in your room in your bed?" I shouted.

"This is my house, and I can do as I please!" She barked back.

I finally had enough and threw the blanket in her face. That was the last straw for Erica. She demanded I get out her house. I would have but my arrogance wouldn't allow me to leave that night. The truth was I had nowhere to go. Instead, I locked myself in Rozlin's room and went to sleep. But I knew my time there was dwindling fast, and it was time to find my own place

The following week, I went apartment hunting. I had never moved into an apartment on my own and didn't really know how the process worked, but I stumbled across an apartment complex that I really liked. I had no credit, but the management agreed to rent to me without pulling a credit report, so I took the apartment. For the first time, I was living on my own.

CHAPTER 11

A Sorry Excuse
for a Son

Moving out of my sister's place, I had no furniture of any sort. All I had to show for myself was a closet full of clothes and shoes. I had enough money to get myself the basics things I needed to survive, but everything hit me at once. I was going through what it felt like to truly be an adult. I realized that, if I was going to fill up the apartment, it was going to be up to my hard work. Walmart and I became best friends. I filled my refrigerator and freezer with Lunchables and Hot Pockets and filled my pantry with ramen noodles. I had no clue how to cook for myself. The first couple of nights were rough because I didn't realize apartments don't come with shower curtains, and the water sprayed all over the bathroom floor. Nevertheless, I could relax on my queen-sized air mattress.

As I became totally independent, I acquired a small mountain of new bills that I wasn't ready to handle. In the beginning of the year, my mother had asked if I wanted to be on her insurance to receive health benefits from her new job. The payment each month was very low, so I said yes, but I had become conditioned to automatic-draft payments that helped me pay my bills on time. I had never paid for health insurance before, so this bill was new for me. A couple months passed, and I hadn't paid my mother for this bill that was being deducted from her check each month. She grew more and more frustrated because she needed every dime of her paycheck.

I figured she could just deduct the money from what she owed me from a $3000 payout I'd received from an investment group, in which I had only invest around $400. She had invested her own money. In fact, she was the one who advised me to get into this investment group because the profits were expected to be seven-fold your original investment. While I was still living in her house, the time had come for me to cash out. My mother took me to go cash my check, but she convinced me she needed the money and would pay me back. She presented it to me as if she and my sisters would be

A Sorry Excuse for a Son

living in a shelter if I didn't help. I felt the responsibility to fill in wherever it was needed to make sure my family was good, and I agreed to lend her the money.

Since she hadn't paid me back by the time I moved out, I told her she could just deduct my health insurance payment from the $3000 she already owed me. That was a slap in the face to my mother, and one day, when I went over to visit, she brought up the subject again. I finally agreed to give her the cash but explained that I would have to make time go to an ATM. She didn't want to hear it.

"Jordan, I need this money," my mother told me. "The company is taking it from my check each month, and I can't afford to not have my entire check right now."

I knew I would get the money to her, so I didn't see what the big deal was. "I'll stop by the ATM when I leave here, but there's no need to get all worked up behind seventy dollars." I told her.

My mother looked at me like I'd just called her a fool to her face. "Don't tell me not to get worked up behind seventy dollars, like it's a small amount. I need all my money, and you're not understanding that."

"Mom, I do understand, but you're yelling and cussing at me, about to ruin our relationship behind that little bit of money. All of this is unnecessary." I didn't understand how disrespectful my explanation was to her, how offended she would be by my assertion that the money shouldn't come between us when, in her eyes, I was the one making it an issue by not paying her.

The argument escalated and resulted in her putting me out of her house and telling me to never come back. Cussing and yelling behind me as I left, she demanded I give her back the key to her house. I didn't feel like the conversation should have resulted in that sort of anger, so I kept walking, but she followed me out the door. I took the key from my keychain as I went.

My mother snatched the key from me. "You're a sorry excuse for a son!" she screamed. "That's why my boyfriend doesn't like your ass in the first place!"

I got in my car and started down the street. I was frustrated, confused, and hurt all at the same time. I wondered how she could have said something like that to me. I was overwhelmed with emotion. I pulled into a driveway around the corner from her house and bawled my eyes out. I couldn't understand what I did to make her feel that way about me, so I called my aunt and explained to her what happened. My aunt was devastated to hear about the argument, but she encouraged me and gave me some advice I'll never forget. "Jordan," she said, "it's okay to love people from a distance, even your mother."

These were hard words for me to swallow because I never wanted any distance between my mother and me, especially after the death of my grandmother, a couple months earlier, which changed things drastically in our family. But I took my aunt's advice. For the rest of the year, I didn't speak to my mother.

• PRINCIPLE •

Evolve Your Self
with Detox

Detoxing wasn't only necessary for my physical health. It was also necessary for my life as a whole. It wasn't enough to simply detox from the food I ate. I had to detox from the music I was listening to, the people in my life, including some friends and family, the church I went to, and the relationships I carried from year to year. I evaluated my entire life, across-the-board, and detoxed in the right areas.

A detox is a process or period of time in which you abstain from and rid your body of toxins or unhealthy substances. When you detox your life, it has to be a holistic process. A true detox doesn't start and end with the food you consume. It includes every area and should produce something new in your life.

I had behaviors, attitudes, and character traits passed down to me from the previous generation. Being parented by my mother deeply influenced who I was. I responded, reacted, and talked like what had been displayed in my life, until I assessed those things and decided which I wanted to keep and which I wanted to lose.

When my mother and I got into a verbal altercation over unpaid bills and she called me a sorry excuse for a son, it pierced my heart and crushed my soul. I couldn't understand why she would allow those words to leave her lips. My aunt explained that I needed to put boundaries around my space and time. I decided to detox from my toxic relationship with my mother, and we didn't speak to each other for an entire year. It hurt, but it was necessary for my growth.

X-ray your life and detox the things that inhibit your growth. This process can't be rushed. It requires time, but it's imperative to creating success in your life. Anything that hinders the time you spend building momentum towards your goal must go. After the toxins are removed, replace them with nourishment. If the music you listen to, the movies you watch on Netflix or even the job you work don't coincide with pursuing your purpose, they're nothing more than a pleasure, and people without purpose seek pleasures to numb pain. They must go!

.

• CHAPTER 12 •

Babylon Has Fallen

Things began to crumble at my church. Our esteemed youth leader, Joel, was accused of molesting a four-year-old girl. This crushing news made headlines in San Antonio. This was a man we had looked up to for so many years. We had spent so much time with him, and never would have assumed a courtroom or prison would be his final destination.

Growing up, I built a strong bond with my church family. I opened up and became vulnerable to the youth leaders and allowed them to speak to me and areas of my life that I'd kept to myself. The only God I knew was through my experiences with them. Nee-Naw had been so sincere in living her life for God, so I figured everybody in the church lived as she did. Church was a place where I could put my guard down and rest on the shoulders of friends who became family.

Joel, the head of the youth department, had the kind of charisma that sucked you in and made you want to participate and engage. In the middle of our home Bible study, Erica once stopped to ask me who my church dad and mom were. She had hers, and mine were always Joel and his wife, Naomi. If I could be raised in any household from the church, I would have chosen theirs.

Joel loved football, boxing, laughing and having a good time. He was seemingly everything I wanted in a father, and over the course of time, he became a father figure to me. The first time I spoke in front of a congregation of people, ever in my life, Joel asked me to speak with him on one of the biggest services of the year, New Year's Eve. In the Black church, this is referred to as "Watch Night Service," and it's an important event. I was honored that he chose me to speak. I spent many nights at Joel's house, playing video games, listening to gospel rap, and enjoying the fruits of what he had built with his family.

Then came the dreadful news. I was in my bedroom at Mom's house, getting ready for bed, when she shouted, "Jordan! Come here!" This wasn't unusual in our household, but I could hear the concern in her voice. I went to her room, where she stared in fascinated shock at the television. The news was on, and the lower-thread read, "Joel Allen, arrested for sexually assaulting a child."

I stood there in disbelief. I couldn't and didn't want to believe what I saw, but the photo of him on the screen told me there was no mistake. Everything I knew to be true shifted and cracked. I was anxious to get back to church just to hear that there was some kind of mistake, but my mother made sure I stayed clear of this allegation and didn't dig too deep. As much as I wanted to come to his defense, I couldn't.

* * *

Because of this disgusting news, the church implemented a new set of strict religious rules that were hard to follow and affected everyone, especially the young people. Church life was no longer about building relationships. Background checks were performed on each of the ministers and leaders in the church. Members blamed our pastor for not knowing the abuse was going on, and many left the church. But when it was time for Joel's sentencing, he insisted the accusation was false and asked anyone who supported him to be there for the hearing.

Joel invited me personally, so I went. As I walked down the court hallways, I felt as if I was getting ready to be charged with something and turned over into the hands of the police. My nervousness, as I walked into the courtroom and saw other members of the church there to support Joel, was gut wrenching. We took our seats on the benches, and the judge called each of our names to make sure we were all in attendance. Court was in session.

Both attorneys presented their arguments for sentencing, and the story began to unfold. When the district attorney unveiled details of the allegations, it finally hit me that maybe Joel was guilty as charged. When I saw that Joel had confessed to the Bexar County Sheriff's office and there was video of his confession, I was shocked. Once the footage was played, I could no longer deny that Joel had done this horrible thing.

I was torn apart. There I stood, in support of him, convinced he would never do something so heinous. I hadn't believed it because, as far as I knew, this man has spent countless years around children and youth without a hint of inappropriate behavior. But I couldn't deny what my eyes had seen and my ears had heard.

Finally, the judge made his final remarks and sentenced our youth leader to nineteen years in prison. The wails from Joel's wife, Naomi, filled the air. Everyone in the room was shaken.

What I'd learned in that courtroom left a bitter taste in my mouth. I wondered if there was anyone I could really trust. I didn't understand what God was doing or why he had allowed so many things to be shaken up in my life. I questioned how I could go to a church where I lacked trust in the leadership. This church had been my foundation. This was the church my grandfather led before passing it to the next pastor, who was still our leader. These were supposed to be my family members. I was closer to them than I was to some people I shared blood with.

Joel had been the youth leader all the young people gravitated to while he was there. The way he positioned himself in the church gave us a unique sense of belonging. Many young people shared countless memories with Joel and preferred him over his second in command. The assistant youth leader had a totally different approach. He and his wife both had a controlling and condescending way of leading the youth. For them, it was all work and no play.

Once Joel was gone, the assistant youth leader took his place. And while he was in leadership, the church lost nearly all the youth who had attended. The excitement and joy of going to church no longer existed. Joel was convicted on November 1, 2014, and from that point on, nothing was the same.

As I made my transition from the youth group to the young adults' class, my pastor recognized my unique leadership qualities and suggested I be mentored by our assistant youth leader. This mentorship and discipleship training would develop me to become a minister. This meant I would be elevated, at a very young age, to a ministerial protocol that brought with it a lot of influence in the church.

The youth leader and I were supposed to work through A Tale of Three Kings together to extract certain principles, but we never met to discuss the book. He neglected to ever call me, and he didn't speak to me when he saw me at church. This was the first of many letdowns. There I was, a passionate and ambitious young man who felt like becoming a minister was my calling in life, and the man who was to mentor me turned his back on me. I couldn't wrap my mind around why he never called me, prayed with me, or took time to show me the ropes.

Nevertheless, I kept the faith. I figured he was too busy and would get to me when he had time. But that time never came. A couple of years later, I attended a men's fellowship at his house. I didn't really want to be there, but I gave it a chance. In front of everyone, he revealed to me why he'd shunned me. He had believed my only mission was a selfish one to continue the legacy of my great-grandfather. With tears in his eyes, he apologized to me, but his confession didn't make me feel any better. It was then I lost trust in my church leadership and their ability to disciple me and bring to fruition the gifts that existed inside of me. I believe the truth was that he wanted to be next up to head the church, and as the only one from my family still going there and participating in church life, he saw me as competition.

This was a critical point in my life because I was finally coming into adulthood and was losing much of what I knew to be true about my church whom I called family. Church rules had become very strict—no R-rated movies, no sports, no Christian hip hop, no makeup or nail polish for women, no jeans, women had to wear long skirts, no swimsuits at the beach, no clothing that could be considered flashy or immodest, and home school your kids. The pastor called these changes Biblical mandates, but I saw them as a means to control. The feelings of family and love were gone. I started meeting with my pastor to try to understand his vision and the direction he wanted for the church because at this point I was conflicted in my soul.

CHAPTER 13

Church Ain't What It Seemed

On a Sunday morning, as I was getting ready for church, I received a call informing me my grandmother was in critical condition. I darted out the door rushing to the hospital. When I arrived, many family and church members were already there with tears in their eyes. Nee-Naw had been admitted to the hospital on multiple occasions, but this time seemed a little different. It was like everybody expected her to pass away. Holding back tears, I looked at her, while she told me one thing I'll never forget. "Trust God," my grandmother said. Those words resounded in me, and will continue to echo, forever and ever.

At the end of 2015, I had lost my best friend, my voice of reason, the matriarch of my family, my grandmother.

After Nee-Naw underwent a double amputation, diabetes caused her great suffering, and ultimately, resulted in her death. This was a rough time because my grandmother was the glue that held us all together. Her love and kindness, relationship with God, and intelligence could touch anyone from a king to a peasant. My mother was the youngest of all my grandmother's children, a mama's girl, which made this journey even more tragic for her and for us.

Right after Nee-Naw died, Erica and I continued to attend the church. But once Nee-Naw was gone, many church members revealed how they really felt about us. The respect and positive energy that once came our way shifted to something unkind. Now we were on the receiving end as other people had been, we noticed how unfairly certain people were treated and how well those favored by our pastor and other ministers were treated. We had fallen out of favor.

* * *

When all else failed, I believed my church family would be there for me. I knew without a doubt in my mind that, regardless of what was going on in my life, my church family would always be solid. I turned to the church for hope and the promise that they could offer me something to fill the hole in my heart. After the fall-out with my mother and the loss of Nee-Naw, I was so confused. I didn't know up from down. All I knew was I wanted some comfort from God and the people who shared a heart for Him.

However, throughout the years the pastor had developed a "restoration process" for big sinner members. They had to go through this process in order to be considered whole again. Essentially, they were isolated from the rest of the church and had to sit through classes to be restored back to regular church functions. I disagreed with this process because the Bible never instructs us to do that.

People who may have fornicated or committed adultery were stuck in this restoration process for however long our pastor and ministers felt was needed. They couldn't attend normal church functions or participate in ministry in any way. Erica and I started to question this and a lot of the church's processes and procedures because we saw they produced negative results and zero effectiveness. I met with our pastor multiple times to make sure I understood his stance on this protocol and to express my concerns about the lack of compassion I observed. His explanations made no sense to me at all.

When I met with the pastor for the last time, he hinted that because I was living a lifestyle that could lead to children being produced out of wedlock, I would have to submit to the restoration process. I refused to do so. I didn't believe the process served to help anyone. Our church mission statement was to bring souls in and send disciples out, but we were doing neither of the two. I didn't want to continue to be a part of a sinking ship that I couldn't save, so after my last meeting with my pastor, we agreed to part ways.

I told the pastor, "You have a family and I have a family, right? You have to do what you think is best for your family, and I have to do what's best for mine."

"So this meeting is concluded," he said.

"Yes, it is," I said. I was angry, but I left the church knowing that, if I had sinned against God, I was already restored in God's eyes. As my relationship with the church came to its inevitable conclusion, I realized religion had given me something to do, not someone to be. The true ministry of outreach and positively impacting and influencing souls didn't happen within the four walls of the church—at least not that church. True ministry, I discovered, takes place by activating your faith and going to the people who need help. I could no longer be fulfilled by the routine of going to a building to praise God. The same Bible we read from, week after week, told us to not just go to church but to be the church. Breaking free of the mental, emotional, and even physical bondage my church had held me in ignited the fire inside me to take my message of freedom, peace, and inspiration to the stages.

I'd been raised through a biased, programed, church based belief system, but I wouldn't continue that legacy. I wouldn't raise my children that way. I never want my children to ever feel the way the pastor made me feel. Instead, I was determined to give my seed someone they could look up to and aspire to be like. I'm committed to giving them an example of a real man in their life. From that day, I knew I would allow my children the freedom to live, to be a human being, and develop their own relationships with God. They would never know the kind of condemnation that came from living under the teachings which I'd been raised.

Evolve Your Self
with Vision

When I was eighteen years old, I reached a breaking point when I went to sleep one night and dreamed about where I wanted to be in my life. After that, I established a solid vision for my life and where I wanted to be by looking at where I did not want to be, examining bad examples in my life and learning from their mistakes.

Vision is the ability to see the end from the beginning. What makes a good barber is the ability to predict the end of a haircut from the beginning, knowing the finish from the start. A good runner knows his race and knows the finish line from the start, which ultimately determines how that runner will run the race. It was imperative for me to see clearly where I wanted to be so I could decide how I would get there.

Vision defined the trajectory I was setting for my life, and everything else in my life that didn't have its place in this vision became a distraction. My goal was to rid myself of every person, place, or thing in my life that was or could be an anchor, holding me down while I was trying to elevate.

The ultimate goal for establishing a solid vision for your life is to understand what you want out of life. What do you want people to say about how you lived from the day you were born to the day you die? Your vision for your life will ultimately create that legacy. We're not created as human beings to do everything but to do some specific thing, and that one thing should not only give meaning and significance to your life but also add value to other people's lives.

Living without vision for your life is like swimming in the ocean. The tides of life will sway you in any direction. Too often we expect life to give us what we want instead of creating our own realities based on our unique vision. You'll never make it to your destination if you don't know where it is. You may have a lot of movement and motion, but you'll rarely see real progress.

Fantasizing won't make manifest your vison. If you don't write your vision on paper and review it often, you cannot expect to run your course accordingly. Write your vision and make it plain. Create a step-by-step plan for how you'll realize your vision. And execute the plan.

Having My Son

Going into 2016, things were rocky for my family. Everyone's emotions were in disarray. Conversation became difficult for us. Any sort of conflict led to months and months of no communication. After a small altercation, my mother and I didn't speak for an entire year. With all I was suffering from losing my grandmother and not speaking to my mother, with all the lies and distrust I had for my home church, I felt alone. I dedicated myself to isolation and staying quiet but still working hard for a year. Each victory in my career went a small way toward filling my well, which was otherwise so dry. All the while, I longed for the love and compassion I'd once gotten from family and church.

I began to look for love in all the wrong places, as the saying goes. I found fulfillment and satisfaction in sex. It was the only thing that made me feel like everything was going to be okay, like someone cared about me, like I was on a fast track to get over this fear that at any moment, I would feel empty again. During this time, I started seeing a young lady whose family owned a daycare next to the barbershop where I worked. I used her to make myself feel better, but I wanted this cycle to stop. I wanted to change and make things right by working on myself.

One night, after I'd gone some time without speaking to her, the young lady called me. My stomach sank when I heard her voice. I'd known my actions would eventually catch up to me. It was just a matter of time. I also knew, if she was calling me, it was something serious, but I answered the phone trying to play it cool. "What's going on?"

"How are you doing?" she mumbled.

"I'm doing all right. Just chillin'. What's up?" I said.

"Well." She paused for a long moment. "I'm pregnant." The conversation continued as I tried to discover her plan of action. It wasn't as if we were in a relationship and had been planning to be together, which would have made the situation better. In fact, we were supposed to be completely done with each other. I was devastated, not because I was going to be a father but because of the unknown and the fears that came along with it.

I didn't know what people—the people at church, my immediate family, my extended family, and especially my mom—would think of me. I didn't want them to cast judgment. Everything was going in my favor in my business and in building my brand, and I wanted nothing to interfere with that. I was all for having a child—but with the woman of my dreams, not with a woman I'd only wanted to have sex with.

After multiple conversations, she made the decision to keep the baby whether I was going to be in his life or not. Not being a father to my child wasn't an option for me. It wasn't in my DNA to be a bad or absent father. I could never allow her to give birth to this baby and not show up 110% as the great father I knew I could be. All my siblings and I were born out of wedlock, and I had never wanted that for my children. That was one family tradition I'd wanted to break, but I had to man up and own my consequences.

I broke the news to my best friends first, friends from church, my boys. While we were headed to the gym one day, I let them know I had a baby on the way. There was a stillness in the car after I made the announcement. We all knew things were shifting. I was entering a different phase in life that required putting childish things behind us. It was time to grow up. "J-Cook," they told me, "We love you and support you. Anything you need, we've got your back." Their positive response lifted a huge burden off my shoulders and gave me some clarity of thought knowing they'd be there through this with me.

Sharing the news with my family was much more difficult because things were already complicated between us, and I felt like I had nowhere to turn. I found out I was going to be a father in February but didn't tell my mother until May. I decided we needed a family sit-down, so I gathered all my sisters and my mother together to break the news.

At this point, because our family was already in shambles, Mom figured we were getting together to discuss how we could improve our relationships. In the past, family meetings had resulted in something horribly negative or terrifically positive, and I imagine she was hoping for the latter. We met at her house, and she called us all to her bedroom. My mom opened the discussion by expressing how she felt about the dysfunction in our immediate family, and we allowed her to get it all off her chest.

Finally, Erica, who I'd already told about the baby, spoke up. "Mom, let Jordan speak. He has something to share with all of us."

My mom looked nervous but she waited for me to have my say, and when I said, "I'm having a baby," she burst into tears. My sisters put their heads down and allowed my mom the space to react. Her reaction wasn't what I'd expected. "You're not going to be anything but a baby daddy!" she screamed at me. I suppose she wanted the best for me, but her reaction made me feel like I had no one in my corner. I wished Nee-Naw was there to give me the comfort and wise words I needed to uplift me.

After that night, I made a decision to deal with the situation on my own. I had no idea how to prepare for my child being born, and by then, I was in a relationship with another girl, and had to break the news to her. I texted: "Hey we need to talk." Right away, she called me on FaceTime. What I had to say was hard but necessary. I told her I was going to be a father.

She looked at me with surprise and hung up the phone in my face. Tears of frustration sprang from my eyes. I had invested everything in this woman, but I had created this situation. I was trying to maintain a relationship with one young lady while another was having my baby.

Evolve Your Self with Peace

Growing up as the only boy of four children to a single mother, in our household, was very difficult. So often, we argued because nobody understood my point of view. I don't know if it was always because I came from a male point of view, but it became very, very frustrating. The toxic things I went through weighed on me. Protecting my peace became another key principle I had to learn in the midst of those dark times in my life.

I struggled for a very long time with performance-based relationships. I thought that, if I performed well enough, people would accept me and I would have peace in my life. If I made everybody happy enough, I thought, it would translate to peace in my mind. But eventually, I grew tired of being tired. I was ready for change. I wanted true happiness in my life. The key was realizing I didn't owe anybody in my life my peace.

First, I had to understand my peace was mine. It wasn't something I was obligated to give someone else. I control me. And with this realization, I no longer gave what was rightfully mine to others to drain.

If you don't have peace of mind, you don't have anything. It does you no good to have $1 million in your bank account, an 850 credit score, and the big house on the hill if you're distraught and everything and everyone in your life is draining your energy. Life can become very daunting and draining, but it's up to you to protect your peace.

Turn up the volume of your inner peace so loud that it drowns out the toxic noise trying to penetrate your soul. Spend time alone. Use that space to get familiar with your triggers or anything that would cause you to revert back into a headspace that isn't conducive to growth. During this time, it's okay to be selfish. Get familiar with you, your weaknesses and strong suits. Before you can conquer any outside adversary trying to attack your peace, you must deal with your inner demons, and that requires dealing with yourself.

Deal with the demons you wrestle with in your own spirit every single day. Demons of insecurity, negativity, fear, unworthiness, rejection, suicidal thoughts, or depression. Face those things. Determine what's acceptable and unacceptable in your life. Establish non-negotiables for the people, places, and things you will entertain.

CHAPTER 15

Stepping into
the Gift

I come from a family of preachers, teachers, and educators who have impacted lives all across the nation. Teaching and leading run in my bloodline. It all started with my great-grandfather Horace M. Young, who was a Bishop in the Pentecostal Assemblies of the World. His legacy, passion, pure and authentic love for God's people run throughout his descendants and were passed down to me.

Growing up in church, I was always captivated by the concept of hope. To see someone who is physically, mentally, and spiritually unable to get free from whatever binds them finally lit up and reignited with joy because of a future hope has always illuminated my heart. That's the great story of Jesus and the cross. He was the sacrificial lamb who tore the veil between us and God to give people, for generations to come hope, like none other. To see someone have faith in what they once did not believe in always gave me an indescribably wonderful feeling.

This feeling derived from a deep desire to see people succeed. I've always had a heart for the hopeless and the lost. Even as a child, I felt an overwhelming sense of compassion and sympathy for any and everybody who needed help. Carrying the message of the gospel that could determine a soul's salvation ignited a fire and passion in me to serve others and save their souls. I loved being the person who taught these lessons and translated this faith into the hearts of every listening ear.

My first time teaching a group of people was at church, where I was selected, out of all the youth, to give a sermon. When I took to the pulpit to deliver this message, I was eleven years old and instantly felt my calling in life. It was a moment of fulfillment. That was where I was supposed to be. At the time, I thought that meant behind the pulpit, preaching to a congregation, using my gift of gab for a higher purpose. I had a fire in my heart to preach and teach with deep conviction, like my great-grandfather and great-uncles had. It felt as if my calling in life and my gifts had aligned, awakening a true passion I hadn't known existed inside me.

Once I left the church, I needed a new way to answer that calling.

One day, soon after I started my barbering journey, a friend who attended cosmetology school at Milan Institute made known to me that the school was inviting guest speakers to come in and educate the students. I'd been speaking and hosting around the city of San Antonio for different organizations and groups, some of which were on college campuses, and I was really honing my speaking skills. I was teaching at University of Texas at San Antonio with a Christian college organization called Aftershock. If I wasn't teaching, I emceed and controlled the flow of each fellowship. My friend put me in contact with the director of the cosmetology school to book what would be my first professional speaking engagement in front of a live audience.

I'd seen other barbers host classes and seminars all across the nation, but I'd never seen anyone use that platform to reach the heart, mind, and soul of each individual in attendance. Their classes were industry specific. They instructed students and professionals on how to become better barbers or stylists, but I wanted my speaking to inspire my audience to become better people. My intention was to fix the broken and heal the hearts of every listening ear, starting with the people in my industry. My goal was to become a beacon of hope for the young and the old by examining my life and extracting keys to success for their personal betterment.

With the lights, cameras, and all eyes watching me, I was a nervous wreck. I couldn't stop shaking as I took the stage. I knew my material because I'd stayed up, night after night, studying and preparing for this moment, but as soon as it came time to deliver, my mind drew a blank. Nevertheless, I introduced myself and delivered each slide on my PowerPoint with as much passion as I could. I was able to push through because, after I introduced myself, one of my slides showed a clip of the video I'd watched each morning as I got ready to go to barber college. After watching that with my audience, I was motivated and amped up to give them this hope that I carried inside. It struck a chord within me, and I remembered why I was there. I could tell by the looks on the faces of the audience that they had never heard a speaker like me. I was twenty years old, delivering my story with inspiration and conviction.

My friend, Kevin was a photographer and videographer, I hired him to record video and photos of the occasion. After the engagement, my friends and I went to eat at Golden Corral to analyze what I'd just done and how it had been received. The feedback I received reinforced my belief that, despite my initial nervousness, I'd done my job well.

Students from the school followed me on social media and sent me messages to thank me for my time and let me know how much I'd inspired them. They loved the determination I had at such a young age. But this was just a first step in the direction I wanted to go. I had been slightly reserved in my delivery, and I would've loved to have given them more energy and more of my personality. I hungered to hit the stage again. I hadn't set out to become a motivational speaker, but by sharing my life's trials, the emotional trauma I'd endured, and how I moved past it all, I developed into what I was always meant to be.

CHAPTER 16

An Entrepreneur Is Born

When I was thirteen years old, I enjoyed going to get a haircut because of the freedom and liberty in the shop. I also appreciated that the barber who cut my hair took the time to teach me a little bit about what it was like to be self-employed. He showed me his clientele book and how much money he was making, and he communicated to me how he was able to do all of this while being self-employed. Right then, I fell in love with the concept of working for myself.

My character, attitude, and ambition weren't suited to having a boss. I never believed in putting all my eggs in a system that wasn't designed for me to succeed, and trust that I would be successful. I hated the idea of working for someone else, and at that age, I hated school, which wasn't designed to help me succeed either. Neither the teachers nor the administrators utilized different teaching strategies to accommodate the unique needs of the children in the classroom. As a result, from elementary school to high school, I struggled. It wasn't that I lacked the smarts to keep up with the other students. It was simply that the public schools were designed to teach and measure success in specific ways. Later, I came to understand they had limited tools for measuring intelligence and anyone who didn't fit within those limits, like me, was pushed aside and overlooked.

I grew disgusted with the teachers. By middle school, I no longer wanted to be confined or bound to school as a means of creating my success. Entrepreneurship and self-employment became my newfound love at fourteen years old. I had seen how the most successful people in my circle, people who had attended college, quit their corporate jobs to pursue their passions as entrepreneurs. They were more successful and they were able to release their true potential by developing their own business ideas. That's what I wanted for my life, and I was going to start as soon as I graduated high school. It was the beginning of entrepreneurship for me.

* * *

The first steps of my entrepreneurial journey began with McCook&Co, and I loved every moment of it. To see my ideas made manifest before me was a dream come true. I attached my brand to any and every piece of merchandise I possibly could, starting with shirts. I ordered black, white, and gold shirts with the McCook&Co. logo on the front. I also handmade and manufactured my own hair pomade for men and women with the help of my two younger sisters, Jaelyn and Amayah.

Alone in my apartment, I studied YouTube videos on how to develop and manufacture my own hair pomade. I wanted something oil based that would add shine and moisturize to my client's hair. Once I had an understanding of what I needed, I ordered everything online, including tin cans to place the product in, bee's wax to solidify it, and raw essential oils. I spent about $50 on materials to develop and package this product, and the return on investment was going to be great, selling sixty-six units at $10 a can.

I became obsessed with numbers, business, and profit. Working in my apartment, my sisters and I used a Pyrex glass to fill each can with the product. We were novices, but determined to get it done. This was the first of many business ventures for me, and I planned to sell the pomade at my brand release party and in my barbershop. This particular business venture wasn't my favorite because I had to manufacture the product on my own, but I had to go through it to learn what worked for me and what didn't. I had ideas for other products I wanted to create, but I didn't find the process fulfilling, so I switched gears. I was ready to move on to the next idea.

* * *

I was determined to become known as one of the hardest working entrepreneurs in the city of San Antonio, and buzz spread across the city about me, my brand, and the work I was putting in to create something special. My barbering schedule filled up fast, and I finally got into my groove. I decided to start cutting hair at six o'clock in the mornings on Fridays and Saturdays to keep up with the clients pouring into my appointment book. Sometimes, I worked a full fifteen-hour day, staying as late as nine o'clock at night.

One Saturday, I had put in about twelve hours when a friend and I decided to go out to eat after work at 54th Street. After knocking back multiple strawberry lemonades, I had to use the restroom, so I excused myself and went. While I was gone from the table, I receive an Instagram direct message from an athlete named

Enzo Amore. The message read: "What's up homey, I hashtagged sanantioniobarbers and found ur page. I don't know what ur day is looking like tomorrow, but if you are around and wanna make some cash if you can cut a few heads in the afternoon at a hotel or something lemme know, we got Monday Night RaW tv show in Houston Monday and I need a fresh cut —- holla."

I was really skeptical. I had never cut anyone's hair in a hotel room before and I had most definitely never cut a WWE Wrestler. I was also puzzled. I kept reading the message over to make sure I was understanding it clearly. The sender's username on Instagram was verified with a blue check, so he was definitely a celebrity. My heart pounded with excitement as I analyzed his account. I couldn't believe this was happening to me.

As I made my way back to the dinner table, I told my friend what happened. She suggested I play it cool and message back, ready to seize the opportunity. So I did. I gave him my cellphone number and told him to text me. We discussed who he was, and after a couple of my questions, he told me to google him. I eventually did, and I began to feel as if this opportunity was legit.

The next morning, I called my younger sister. "Jaelyn," I said, "You won't believe what's happening right now!"

She answered nonchalantly, "What?"

"WWE superstar Enzo Amore hit me up and wants me to cut his hair before his wrestling match on national television!" I screamed.

I asked her to go with me to the hotel as a precaution. (Some big brother! But Jaelyn was tough, and if I was being scammed, she'd have my back.) That morning, I rushed to the shop to clean and pack all my tools. I was extremely excited but still somewhat skeptical, but I darted to my mother's house to pick up Jaelyn. I was honking, blasting my music, and she could tell I was really excited. We both were.

We followed GPS to a hotel near the airport, more and more, the opportunity began to feel legit. We finally arrived and followed the instructions given to us in the text messages to find his room. I really didn't know what to expect because I wasn't a fan of the WWE and had never watched it growing up, but apparently, Enzo Amore and his partner, Big Cass, were a big deal.

When we arrived on the fourth floor, the ding from the elevator seemed to last an entire minute. My nerves were in a complete disarray as we made our way down the hallway, adjusting our shirts and outfits to make sure our swag was right. We wanted to be presentable, but at the same time we were preparing to be abducted by strangers. I knocked on the door, staring my sister straight in the eyes. My heart pounded out my chest and my stomach flipped over.

The door opened, and there stood a five-foot-ten-inch muscle man with a leopard print design colored in the sides of his head and a highlighter blonde Mohawk that had been straightened so it flowed with the slightest breeze. In a deep, scratchy voice, he said. "What's up, guys? You must be Jordan."

"Yes," I said, "and this is my sister Jaelyn here to help me out today." The fear of being kidnapped had gone away, but I was still nervous about giving him a great haircut for the event. Fortunately, I was able to do my best work and give the wrestlers what they wanted, and the experience was eye-opening. It propelled me to continue to strategically put myself out there where opportunity could find me.

* * *

My reputation as an inspiring speaker was growing around San Antonio. Add to that I was winning barber competitions and had the success of McCook&Co. merchandise, and people began to attach a face to my name. I had hired a couple friends to work part time for me, and one of their initiatives was to reach out to local radio stations to inquire about advertising opportunities. The plan was, while I was working in the barbershop servicing clients, I would have a team of individuals reaching out to promote and market me and my brand.

While working in the barbershop one day, I received a call from my sister, who was one of the people I'd hired to work on my behalf. When she called to update me on what was going on, I heard the excitement in her voice. "Jordan, the people at 930 AM, the answer radio station, want to sit down and have a meeting with you!" she said. They wanted me to meet with their board of executives to discuss my vision for my career and business along with potential opportunities to work together. It seemed they had a big vision for their radio station as well.

I was focused on becoming more than a barber who cut hair behind the chair. I wanted to expand my brand and push the limits to see how far I could go, so I was ecstatic about the opportunity. Barbering was cool, but I was also motivated by the additional opportunities barbering created for me. And this was a step in that direction, allowing me to expand to greater markets. It was my job, then, to call the station and close the deal.

After wrapping up servicing the client in my chair, I jumped on that call, and we arranged a meeting.

On the day of the meeting with the radio station, I was excited and nervous as I dressed in my business attire. There I was, just twenty-one years of age, getting ready to negotiate a contract with a major radio station for my business. Dress shoes and collared shirt on and pen and notebook in hand, I made my way to the station's building. While I rode the elevator up, I rehearsed my pitch over and over again to make sure I was well-equipped for whatever was thrown my way.

At the front desk, the receptionist, a pleasant woman, said softly, "You must be Jordan McCook."

It made me feel extraordinarily good to be greeted in such a way, as if I was someone she should know. She offered me water and walked me into a conference room with a long table surrounded by office chairs. This was a totally new experience for me, and I was elated to be there.

By the end of the day, a representative, who would ultimately become the executive over my show, offered me the chance to host my own hour-long show on their radio station. I had never dreamed of becoming a radio personality, but I was intrigued by successful radio hosts, like Sway Calloway of Sway in the Morning and Steve Harvey of The Steve Harvey Morning Show. I would develop content and host my own show, which would play on Saturdays with over 100,000 listeners every week. How could I turn it down? It aligned with my brand and what I wanted to represent as an entrepreneur: trying new things and really pushing the limits, challenging myself beyond measure.

* * *

I worked diligently with my team to bring my radio show to life. We even went so far as to bring in our own camera crew to shoot the radio show and post the videos on YouTube. Entertainment was a completely new field for me, but I loved every bit of it. I had never seen anyone in my life carry this kind of responsibility, but I was motivated to learn how to do it. Every day was a grind, but carrying camera equipment and the backdrop onto the elevator to ride up to the studio gave me a rush. I was dedicated and committed to the grind and to putting out excellent work.

My goal for the show was in alignment with my mission statement and brand, to represent an outward expression of an internal greatness. I interviewed a lot of San Antonio influencers who put in work and created great success for themselves in their fields. I provided a platform for them to share their life experiences and promote their music, books, or brands. Since I was still heavily involved in the church at this time, a lot of my guests came from my church and other churches in the area. I also targeted major influencers in music, and this helped my show build enough hype to be invited to South by Southwest Conference and Festivals (SXSW), an annual conglomerate of film, interactive media, music festivals, and speaker sessions that takes place in mid-March Austin, Texas yearly. The event began in 1987 and has continued to grow in scope and variety every year, becoming one of the most prestigious events of its kind.

I wrestled with the idea of participating in South by Southwest for a while because it would require me to travel about eighty miles from San Antonio to Austin, and I'd have to haul a ton of equipment to the venue. But it was an opportunity other radio show hosts, entertainers, and businesspeople dreamed of landing. I accepted the challenge and got busy searching San Antonio for a business that leased studio equipment. After several days of research, I stumbled across a credible business in San Antonio. I met with John from Momar Music, and he cut me a deal on the exact equipment I needed. John gave me an unbeatable price, which made the experience all the better.

Anticipation and excitement carried me along as the days went by and the festival approached. Finally, the weekend of the event arrived. I'd need to be in Austin Friday, Saturday, and Sunday, and anybody privy to the workings of a barbershop knows these are the busiest days of the week for us. But I was willing to sacrifice the money I would have made in the barbershop that weekend to be a part of South by Southwest. I wanted to push the limits to see just how far I could expand my horizons with my radio show.

I'd hired a crew of three cameramen to meet me at the festival to shoot the entire event. My head photographer, who did the filming and editing when we shot in the studio, would direct. That made for a total of four on the photo-video crew. Joining us also was a friend of mine from church named Trent. He had the type of personality that would go great with the radio show and make each guest feel comfortable. Trent and Kevin, who was shooting video, and I loaded up one car and made our way to the great city of Austin, Texas.

Down I-35 we went. Along the way, we made one stop at P. Terry's Burger Stand, one of our favorite burger spots, which we didn't have in San Antonio. As we got back on the highway filled with so many cars, the rush of the moment finally hit me. I rolled down the back window, stuck my head out, and screamed, "South by South West!" As I was doing so, my hat flew off my head and down the highway. The hat was a gift to me from my girlfriend at the time, and I wanted to wear it for the radio show filming. I couldn't help laughing at myself out of sheer embarrassment. We made a detour back to where I thought I'd lost my hat, and I found it on the highway, flattened and covered with tire marks and dirt. It was pure comedy, but it all made for a great experience. Laughing, we got back in the car and headed to the venue.

The parking lot was empty as we pulled in, and I wondered if we were at the wrong venue. I called one of the executives to confirm we were at the right spot, and it turned out he had change the date of the event. We were a day early, but we decided to stay in Austin and enjoy the festivities. The streets were filled with people eating, drinking, listening to music, and attending different events. This was a first-time experience for all three of us, and we made the most of it.

The next day, we were ready and excited to set up at the event and catch it all on camera. When we arrived, we were greeted by the event coordinator and his staff in a fashion that made us feel like we were the celebrities. I could hear the music and commotion going on behind the double doors inside the venue. As we walked in, I stared all the way down to the stage, where a huge screen showed graphics of the artist who would perform that evening. Vendors sold T-shirts and other merchandise for the artists.

I was escorted backstage, where I'd set up and conduct my interviews. We were allowed to set up in the largest area possible, which made me feel good since we were the youngest radio show in attendance. It turned out, we had one of the most dynamic setups at the entire event. Instead of just having a backdrop and a mic for interviews, we had three mics, lights, four cameramen, and our own radio show T-shirts to hand to each artist after an interview. We were creating an experience with the artist they wouldn't forget. We were selected to interview some of the biggest names performing for the weekend. We interview Sunday's Best runner-up Alexis Spight, Sunday's Best winner Joshua Rodgers, gospel hip-hop artist Eshon Burgundy, along with artist and entrepreneur AJ McQueen. These interviews aired on our McCook&Co. Radio Show channel.

As the days went on, I thought of how I'd started off as a barber, cutting hair behind the chair, moved on to hosting different speaking engagements around the city, and now had a radio show. I was motivated by the process and the work I'd put in to be there. When it was all said and done, my show received a ton of publicity around the city and beyond. Many of the artists I connected with at SXSW spread the word about my radio show through their own social media, and showed their support by posting pictures of themselves wearing our promotional t-shirt. From my perspective, the event was a complete success.

· PRINCIPLE ·

Evolve Your Self with Only Quality Product (OQP)

When I began my business, I made a decision to only put out quality product. Your product is your produce. It's the food your customers will consume from you. And all it takes is one case of food poisoning for people to decide they'll never eat from your table again.

When I started cutting hair, I compared the work I put forth to the work of the barbers and stylists whose work I admired. I didn't fool myself into believing, because I was my mother's child, my work was automatically special and comparable to the quality of work others put out. I was honest and true in my assessment of my work and committed myself to only putting out quality product. This included holding myself accountable to honing my craft each day, one YouTube video at a time.

No matter what the product was, I was committed to quality work from McCook&Co. If it didn't make me say "Wow!" I wouldn't release or display the product for the world to see. I wanted my brand to embody youthfulness and excellence at the same time. That included my social media profiles, my websites, my business cards, and any social media posts. This standard required me to invest a lot of money in quality video work, quality editors, and quality photographers, who created the overall look and character I wanted to portray for the world to see.

Stop allowing other people and yourself to misrepresent the essence of the brand you want to portray to the world. Instead, identify what your target audience and potential customers desire and craft your brand accordingly. Don't compare yourself to the unfinished brand or business your friend may have started years ago but never developed into anything. Compare your brand to those that are nationally recognized and critically acclaimed. Set the bar high.

CHAPTER 17

Life Changes

On September 22, 2017, my son was born.

To many people, this would be a glorious moment, but I felt conflicted. I was at the highest point of my life, all the while feeling like it was the lowest. At twenty-one years old, I was split between wanting to be the best father I could possibly be and wondering, "Is this girl really giving birth to my baby?" I'd been influenced by the thoughts of my mother and siblings as to the possibility that this child wasn't mine, and I wrestled with that possibility through the entire pregnancy. It didn't help that my girlfriend didn't understand why I would even consider being in the delivery room when I wasn't sure the baby was mine. After multiple arguments with her, I made the decision to be there to witness my son coming into this world.

The experience was nothing like I thought it would be, but it was magical. Around nine o'clock at night, I got the call and I dropped everything. I called my mother and let her know my baby's mother was being induced. I also called my closest friend and discussed with him the excitement and nervousness I felt. Mom and my aunt Debbie rushed to the hospital, meeting me there, and seeing their faces gave me the courage I needed in that moment.

The birthing room was very quiet as we waited hours for the process to start. I grew hungry and decided to go downstairs to grab some food, and of course, while I was down there eating, I received a text message letting me know her water had broken. I had no idea what that meant, but in my mind, the baby was on the way.

I headed back up to the birthing room, where the process was moving along, and finally, the doctor came in and told her to get ready to push. I took my position and grabbed her left leg to assist her. "One, two, three!" the doctor said over and over again, and each time, I pushed her legs to make the process easier. Lo and behold, after a few of pushes, the baby arrived.

It was one of the most beautiful yet horrifying sights I'd ever seen. A sense of pride washed over me. I was a father, and I was prepared to give my son everything

I'd missed out on as a child. I didn't want to leave the hospital to go to work or anywhere else. I just wanted to be there for my son in that moment and for the rest of my life.

*   *   *

I'd always wanted to purchase my first house before I was twenty-five years old. I didn't know how I would do it or what house it would be, but I held on to my goal. I was living in a two-bedroom apartment at the time and was comfortable with my living space, but when my lease was up, it was time for me to make arrangements for my living situation. Because I was so busy and didn't have the time to go out and apartment hunt, as my lease ended, I had nowhere to stay. Still, I didn't want to renew my lease at the same apartment complex. I was ready for change.

I needed a place to stay, but there was no way I could go back to live with my mother. She would have opened her doors and allowed me to live with her, but living with her as her adult child came with a heap of headaches and friction. She had a rough time respecting the fact that her kids had grown up. Instead, I asked my grandmother on my father's side of the family if I could move in with her for a short time while I sorted out my situation. I wasn't looking to live there permanently, just long enough to get my feet underneath me and find a new place.

I had to be out of the apartment by Tuesday of the following week, and on Thursday, I received a call from my grandmother letting me know I couldn't live with her. She told me I needed to make things right with my mother instead. She'd agreed and then backed out at the last minute, so I had to make some quick adjustments to my plan. That weekend, I had no idea what I was going to do or where I would live. However, a man who had taken me under his wing while I was in church, Reggie, told me he had a house for rent and he really wanted me to take the space.

I had inquired about living there before, but it had never been a serious discussion. Then, the guy he'd agreed to allow to stay in his house disrespected him, so Reggie gave me a call on that Sunday, two days before I had to be out of my apartment, telling me the house was open and I could move in. I was still renting, but I was okay with that. A guy from my church lived with me at the time, so we could split rent down the middle and live in a bigger and better space. I wanted my son to grow up in a house, and I was excited to be able to give him that even if I didn't own it yet.

After several conversations, Reggie told me he wanted to sell the house, and I made arrangements to buy it. As a child I'd heard my mother talk about stability and establishing memories in a home instead of jumping from apartment to apartment. That's what I wanted for my son and my family, a sense of home. So, at twenty-two years old, I began purchasing my first property.

Evolve Your Self with Fatherhood

Have you ever wondered why you get your last name from your father? It's one of those realities of life that few people question. My theory is your father is the measuring tool for your identity. If you're a man who hasn't become a father or never had your father, think of the fathers in your life as you read this, and see how the lessons I've learned can help you better understand or relate to them. If you're a woman reading this, know that I appreciate the role of mother as essential too.

Since my father was absent, my mother became the only father I knew. This meant my perception of who I was to become was one-sided, which caused an emotional and psychological imbalance in my life. Fatherlessness left many holes in who I was. I often blamed my mom. It wasn't her fault, but I directed my misplaced anger toward her. My mother was there, but it takes a man to raise a man. She did the best she could, but too often, she lacked understanding when it came to who I was and who I was becoming.

I turned to my heavenly Father, but I only knew Him through the men in my church, who were incapable of filling this empty vessel. They lacked the capacity within themselves to truly nurture and develop my lost soul. Religion gave me something to do, not someone to be. So, through my hardships, I began to father myself.

I never knew fatherhood would be so near and dear to my heart, but it has become one of the most important roles I fulfill in my life. Growing up, I watched the memorable, heartbreaking scene of Fresh Prince of Bel Air, in which Will Smith's character breaks down after his father once again runs out on him. His feelings of abandonment, brokenness, and loss were real to me. I couldn't understand how a man could bring a child into this world and go on living life as if he has no duty or responsibility to raise his child. It struck me to the core because, as my mother's only son, I wanted someone there who could take my side, understand where I was coming from, and be there to guide me through the problems I faced as a young boy becoming a man.

When I found out I was having my first child, I was astonished to find out it was a boy. My firstborn would be my son.

Before my son was born, I began to really explore this idea of fatherhood long before his birth. I realized that, beyond fatherhood being my duty and responsibility to my son, there was a deeper and more significant meaning to it all. I often questioned God, asking how a fatherless boy was now to become a father. I didn't have one, but now I had to be one. There were so many people I wanted to talk to about this, but I felt as if no one in my life would understand. It was a journey I had to travel by myself. I bore, and continue to bear, the heavy load that comes with fatherlessness.

Fatherhood has changed me. As a child I didn't have the answers for how to become a man or what that meant, but for my son, I now know what to do. I learned by seeing what not to do. I learned from what I missed in my own upbringing. I realize now that fatherhood is one of the greatest callings God has placed on my life. I realize now that my son will have a Bible, blueprint, and source on how to become a man. He will always have a father in his life. It's my job and my responsibility to define what it means to be a father.

father: source, nourisher, sustainer and provider, protector, foundation, and friend

It's hard to know who you are if you struggle to identify the source of where you are from. If you don't know who you are or where you're from, you will fail at finding where you're going in life. A nourisher will give you the proper sustenance, allowing you to unleash your full potential. As a father, you can't parent each child the same. You must customize each level of sustenance so the child becomes tailor made. When you're tailor-made, it's impossible to fit in, thus eliminating the desire for unnecessary approval and validation.

The sustainer is one who helps you embrace the chaos of a storm and prevails in the end. As a sustainer, you uphold the integrity of your position regardless of how hard the winds blow. You're the support where there is none, the backbone, the strength that affirms the validity. As a father, serving as your child's protector isn't just about exercising your "macho." It's being the hedge of protection around your child through prayer, education, and understanding. Knowledge and wisdom performs miracles when your strength can't. A father should shield and safeguard his child's innocence.

As the founder in a child's life, a father must be the solid rock on which the child can build. without a solid foundation there can be no elevation! Without that foundation, the child is subject to making impulsive decisions and succumbing to pitfalls. Without that foundation, the child may well lack a connection to his or her authentic self.

Finally, a friend is more than a title. They say a friend sticks closer than a brother. True friends allow you to express your thoughts and feelings and be your full self in their presence. A father who can be a friend, becomes the child's wellspring of validation and approval. A father serves his child best, not as a dictator, not as a lord, but as a true friend.

CHAPTER 18

Everybody Can't Go Where You're Growing

From a young age, I had a vision inspired by Floyd Mayweather Jr and the way he organized his business. When I created McCook Promotions Enterprises, my goal was to bring together a group of driven and committed young entrepreneurs who wanted to take their businesses and their dreams to the next level. I figured I could start this thing with close friends and colleagues and expand from there. I was determined to inspire and motivate them to become entrepreneurs and chase their dreams. They saw how committed I was to building my empire from the ground up. They saw my game and my struggles. My belief was that they would absolutely want to be a part of this movement. Their support of my dreams would in return support their own dreams. I wanted to throw entrepreneurship on any and everybody who came close to me.

To get everyone to buy into my idea, I invited my friends to a meeting at Starbucks. I wanted to bring this dream to reality with Anthony, aka Pop, Jay, Darius, Whitney, Cierra, and Gabby. It was January of 2018, and I was beginning my speaking tour for the year. I laid out the upcoming events. I wanted them to travel with me and represent this great brand I was building. We would become an amazing unit of young entrepreneurs relentlessly chasing their passions in life. Their dedication to me would be matched by my dedication and commitment to making their dreams a reality. Pop wanted to be a model, Jay had dreams of becoming a graphic designer, and the others were trying to figure it out, but we banded together to support one another's dreams and goals to the best of our abilities.

Everyone was on board, and we all shared the same vison. Our first trip to Paul Mitchell, in Dallas, where I would speak to the students, was quickly approaching, and each individual had a responsibility to make the trip flow as smoothly as possible. Team members were assigned to reserve the rental car, book the Airbnb, and make sure our video presentation was prepared and our merchandise table was squared away at the venue. This was a dream come true for me, not only because I got to travel with my closest friends, but because each of them played a crucial role in making it all happen. I saw the light in their eyes as we brought the vision closer to a reality.

Things flowed so smoothly on our way to Dallas. However, after driving four hours, the GPS took us off the highway and down a long, dark road that gave us all an eerie feeling. We went from jamming music, laughing, and dancing to everyone getting still and observing what was going on around us. I was driving, so I turned down the music and asked, "Is anyone else seeing what I'm seeing?"

Everyone laughed nervously, and we continued to follow the directions of the GPS. No street lights, only a few residents had on their porch lights—the vibe was altogether creepy. We arrived at the rental we'd booked at eleven o'clock at night. Inside, it looked like an old house someone had been murdered in. I was certain we were being watched on cameras. It felt way too much like we'd stepped into a scary movie.

We were all skeptical of the neighborhood and the look of the place, but we were hungry and decided on Waffle House for dinner. When we got back to the Airbnb after eating, we agreed to sleep in close quarters to keep each other safe. We were completely unfamiliar with this neighborhood and didn't want this to be the trip where we all died. It was comical, in the morning, to think about how afraid we'd been the night before, but in the moment, it wasn't funny at all.

By the time the trip was over and we headed back home, I felt like a complete failure. As a team, we weren't in unison. Onstage, I had delivered my presentation passionately, and I was pleased with my message, but there was friction between two of my friends, who were a couple. They argued the entire time and made the experience hell for the rest of us. I searched for ways to correct things when I got back home, but people had their own lives and other things they wanted to do. Almost as soon as I'd brought it together, the team was showing cracks.

I hadn't realized that working with those closest to you could be so difficult. We all had good intentions, but a long list of personal issues affected our ability to work together. For me, this was all business. It was time to take my speaking career into my own hands and push the pedal to the metal, but for some of them, this was merely another job. I wanted to create a space where they could fully invest themselves in themselves. I thought they would see me living out my dreams in the work I put forth to make this thing come true, and we would work together to create the same for them. But that's not what happened.

Some of my friends complained because they weren't being compensated for the trips. They wanted to get paid for these engagements. They didn't understand that my speaking engagements weren't yet paid gigs. I was covering all the travel expenses for the entire team. I even paid for us to all go out to eat after local events. That was my deal with them, and even though it seemed like we were all on the same page, apparently that wasn't the case. Eventually, the team broke up, like a bad R&B group, and we all went our separate ways.

* * *

"Touching More Hearts Than Heads" has been and will always be the heartbeat of McCook&Co. Like LeBron is more than an athlete, I wanted to be more than a barber. From my digital mentors, I learned that anyone who was truly great in history invested in others. The mission of touching more hearts than heads was derived from a place of wanting to positively impact, inspire, and influence lives all across the world through the gifts manifested in me by God.

I cut a ton of hair, and I was determined to advance my career as a speaker at the same time. I've always had a heart for the people, and using the gift of gab that God gave me, I planned to inspire others to become the best versions of themselves. I was motivated to begin my tour all across the nation by getting booked at various venues. The tour would be entitled "Touching More Hearts Than Heads, Volume One." Speaking at schools around San Antonio, I was committed to expanding this message of hope to every listening ear.

I traveled to speak at various cosmetology schools because I wanted to start in the industry where I had the most influence and which provided the biggest platform for me. I had never booked a speaking engagement out of the state, so for the first year on tour, I wanted to land an out-of-state gig. I never set out to be a motivational speaker. That title always seemed corny to me. I thought many motivational speakers came across as too programmed and their message was often so cliché. But my motivation was my story.

Getting onstage in front of all those people and giving hope to them at times when I didn't have hope or belief in myself, was my therapy. I told my story and shared the traumatic experiences I'd been through in hopes that one life would be touched, ultimately honing in on the slogan, "touching more hearts than heads." Sharing my struggles and experiences had a real impact on the students at the cosmetology schools.

After leaving each school, inbox messages flooded my social media. So many students thanked me for sharing my story because they'd been through the same or similar experiences. Some had undergone experiences even more traumatic than my own, and yet they continued to wake up each and every day and press toward their dreams and goals.

What they didn't understand was that, as I poured my heart out to each of them onstage and motivated them, their testimonies motivated and inspired me. They were the fuel I needed in my quest to become more than a barber. I had no formal training on how to book speaking engagements or even how to compose a proper email, but I researched and found the knowledge I needed because I was absolutely hungry for success. I dedicated and committed myself to excellence and to becoming the best speaker and barber I could possibly be so my light could shine and make manifest the greatness inside me in service to others.

My mother had always encouraged me not to be content with staying in the city of San Antonio, and traveling gave me the rush and thrill I'd been searching for all along. In the first year of touring and traveling the nation on my own dime, I not only booked my first out-of-state speaking engagement, but I was also able to travel all the way to Toronto, Canada, with one of the industry leaders, who became a great friend to me, Corey Bonez, Da Goat.

*   *   *

This was a very exciting time for me because I never thought my story, my business, and my influence could travel beyond my community and my state. I spent countless hours calling various schools to find a way in to share my story. I called the front desks of several Paul Mitchell Schools trying to get booked as a guest artist, I let them know I was willing to travel to the school on my own dime. The Paul Mitchell School in Atlanta, Georgia, was the first to allow me this opportunity.

To promote this huge milestone in my career, I contacted my digital graphic designer to put together a flyer letting everyone know I was traveling to my first out-of-state speaking engagement. I shared the flyer on all of my social media platforms. I wanted my family, friends, and support system to see my growth and how hard I was working in silence to produce real results.

I had to pay my own way to Atlanta, but that didn't bother me. It was all a part of a long-range plan. I arrived late at night and prepared to speak the next morning. I'd hired a camera crew to capture the moment for me, and I was looking forward to it. I woke up early that morning, drank my coffee, and left the hotel in an Uber, but when I arrived at the school, I was confronted by puzzled faces. I had arrived late. I was completely unaware of the time difference. Atlanta was an hour ahead of San Antonio, and I had missed the mark. I had two hours scheduled for my entire engagement and I was forty-five minutes late.

The learning leader greeted me with an attitude of disdain and, without saying so directly, made it clear he hadn't wanted me there in the first place. I wasn't used to that kind of treatment because everyone in San Antonio always greeted me with smiles and open arms. This experience was totally different, but the setbacks didn't defeat me. They only motivated me to go harder. The learning leader asked me, "Do you still want to speak today, or do you just want to go back to the hotel?" My answer: "Of course I want to speak today! I didn't come all the way to Atlanta not to!"

I connected my laptop to their TVs, so my presentation would play on the big screens, and made my way to the stage. If I wasn't able to do the entire haircut demonstration, I thought, at least I could introduce myself, motivate and inspire, and get out of their hair. I delivered my presentation passionately and with all the energy I had to give. I poured my heart out to the students, telling my story and revealing my scars to positively impact them. Perhaps I could have impressed them by listing my accolades and accomplishments, but I felt it would penetrate their heart and souls more if I detailed what I'd been through and how I was overcoming. I was pleased with the overall response I got from the crowd. After the learning leader rushed me off the stage, the students had my back. They made it known that they wanted me to stay.

I spent the rest of my time in Atlanta touring the city on my own, going to places like World of Coca-Cola, Georgia Aquarium, and one of the best soul food restaurants, Busy Bee Cafe. As I maneuvered through the streets of the ATL, I reflected on my experience. From Uber rides to time spent alone in my hotel room and my moment on stage, I was so grateful for how far God had brought me. My dreams were really becoming a reality right before my eyes.

Later, I hit my knees and thanked God for every low I'd been through that made this high so fulfilling. The satisfaction of knowing I was operating in my God-given calling was heaven on Earth to me. Some people may have feared stepping out into an unfamiliar city on their own, but not me, I embraced it. I believed in my higher calling and set out to achieve what God had set before me. This was my destiny and this speaking engagement would be the first of many.

* * *

Throughout my career, I've been aware of barber celebrities and barbering influencers who have thousands upon thousands of followers. On my quest to become more than a barber, I began tagging some of these people on my social media posts. On April 3, 2018, I received a message from one of the barbers I'd tagged, BonezDaGoat. The message read: "Keep it up my guy well done 👌■." I responded: "Bro, you're literally one of my favorite barbers and I definitely didn't think you'd see my vid. Your work inspires me every day! Thanks g🙏■." This was a dream come true. As a young barber in the industry, I admired BonezDaGoat, and I was thrilled to know one of the greats was finally recognizing me for my work.

Around this time, the barber college I'd attended was hosting its second annual barber battle, and they invited judges from all over the United States and Canada to participate. I was on a quest to attain everything the industry had to offer, so I competed in the battle. There was a meet-and-greet at Alamo City Barber College where contestants rubbed elbows with the judges. It was a rare opportunity to network and connect with some of the people I looked up to and aspired to be like.

During the meet-and-greet, I got a chance to speak to Lena Piccininni about her life and had a heartfelt conversation with her. I assumed, because of her prestige in the industry, that she would be stuck-up. But I totally misjudged her. She spoke openly with me and gave me the raw and uncut version of her story. We both held back tears as we kicked open the back door to our lives and shared how far we'd come. My view of her completely changed and my respect for all that she'd accomplished grew. For the first time, I saw these celebrities as real people, and in doing so, I was able to connect with some of them, including Scott "Famos" Ramos, on a deeper level. I also had a huge win at the battle and walked away with a $2000 prize.

A couple months later, I was booked to speak in Miami, where I would teach two classes at a Paul Mitchell School. I reached out to Bonez, a Florida native, to see if he knew a photographer or videographer I could hire to capture these moments. He connected me with a videographer who was a good friend of his. That was a small step in building a relationship with Bonez, but I realized it was imperative that I go the extra mile to cultivate that relationship while I was there. It was important to show my commitment and hunger. If Bonez had any opportunities for me, I'd be ready.

In an effort to build on our connection and get to know him better, I booked a haircut with Bonez the day before my class. Throughout our conversation, I noticed a lot of similarities between us, and I began to appreciate him and the opportunity to learn from him even more. He mentioned to me that he was speaking at a large barber expo in Toronto, and invited me to attend. In that moment, the world stopped and I felt the thrill of excitement rising from my toes! I didn't let my response show, but I was jumping up and down inside.

The expo was just four months away, but I had one big problem, I had no passport. I had never traveled out of the country. When I arrived home from Florida, I immediately got on the phone to figure out how to get my passport expedited. I found out the passport office was located in Houston, only two and a half hours from me. "Perfect!" I thought. I scheduled my appointment, went in to apply, and waited patiently for my passport to arrive in the mail. Receiving it a week later was a dream come true. I was ready. My flight was booked and my clothes were picked out. I was ready to experience an amazing show.

I knew many great industry leaders would be there, but I wasn't sure exactly who they would be. Still, I was motivated to be in that atmosphere as Bonez's plus-one.

I landed at the airport in Toronto and was shocked to see everything written in French. I tried to read the signs using my two years of high school French, but I ended up following the crowd. By the time I finally arrived at the hotel, I was exhausted from a day of travel and just wanted to relax.

I got a chance to take a nap, then venture around the city on my own a bit. I was hungry, so I walked a couple miles from my hotel to a familiar restaurant, Red Lobster. Walking to and from, I witnessed so much. The culture of Toronto seemed so free. Everyone seemed liberated from stress or worries. It was a partly cloudy day outside, but that didn't stop a parade of nearly ten thousand people from rolling down the streets singing praises to Jesus. I'd never seen anything like it, so I pulled out my phone and started to record. People of all races gathered, smiling from ear to ear, dancing and singing songs to God while playing instruments. Trucks carried people and blasted gospel music from speakers mounted to the sides of the vehicles. It was a unique and amazing experience, not like anything I'd ever seen on a normal workday in the United States.

Later that evening, Bonez arrived, and we moved around the hotel together, meeting up with other barbers. Going into one hotel room, Bonez introduced me to a good friend of his, Diego. After meeting Diego, I clicked on his Instagram to follow him and noticed he had 149,000 followers. Obviously, he was an influencer in our industry. Later, Bonez shared with me that Diego was one of the top branded barbers in the industry. I could learn a lot from him.

Other barbers trickled in, and I met them one by one. Among these, the last to arrive was Scott "Famos" Ramos. We locked eyes, and he stared at me in disbelief. "What's up, bro!" I said. "I told you you'd see me again." He was shocked, and so was I. He hadn't expected to see me, and I hadn't known I could so quickly be in the same room with barbers I idolized. My idols had now become friends and would become business partners.

At the expo, I saw so many industry greats in one space, performing at the highest levels. I was also invited to teach a haircutting class and tag team a haircut with Famos. By the end of the night, I'd shared the stage with some of the most amazing barbers and stylists in the world. There were about three thousand people in the audience, and they all celebrated as the ten of us closed out the night onstage, cheering for each other and for our industry.

• PRINCIPLE •

Evolve Your Self with Only Quality People (OQP)

Renowned motivational speaker Les Brown, one of my digital mentors, taught me that everybody in my life can't go where I'm growing. As a child who was often left feeling lonely, abandoned, and forgotten, it was easy for me to want to fill my life with people. Having people close to me gave me the security and comfortability I yearned to have. I wanted and needed the affirmations of other people to make me feel good about everything going on in my life. The success I was achieving, my relationship with my son, and my business endeavors, all needed validation from other people, so I surrounded myself with people who could offer that validation.

At that time, I only vibrated at a frequency that allowed me to produce to the level of my surroundings. But once I began to look for validation internally instead of externally, I freed myself from being locked into performing to the level of people my same age from the same place as I was from. My measuring stick became the person I was yesterday. I moved fearlessly, unafraid to grab every challenge by the throat and pursue the life I deserved to live.

When you're liberated from your own fears, you unconsciously give people permission to free themselves. When you value your life, you only allow people in your circle who offer equal or greater value. I stopped taking advice from people who I wouldn't trade places with in life. I surrounded myself with quality people. Certain friends and their old habits had become toxic to my growth. Some family members could no longer climb to the mountaintop with me. However, cutting them off wasn't the hard part. The hard part was learning to be okay with my time alone.

I dedicated a year of my life to getting to know myself. I began to place a higher level of value on my life. I realized the true value I have to offer the world, and with that change I paid more attention to who I allowed in my circle.

Examine and assess the five to ten people you associate with most. Ask yourself if they're living the kind of life you want for yourself. It may sound harsh and insensitive, but if you have to, break free from anyone who's stifling your progress. If you hang out with nine losers in your life, chances are you are the tenth!

CHAPTER 19

Next Level

While I was touring from city to city, speak at various Paul Mitchell schools, I discovered a way to get paid for each engagement within the Paul Mitchell systems. I spent countless hours networking and inboxing different people on social platforms to open doors for me to have a chance to be a paid speaker. I heard no a ton of times, but the search was for one yes.

I wanted to expand my brand and who I was as a speaker so much so I had traveled all the way to Miami, Florida, to speak at the Paul Mitchell school there. On my way from Fort Lauderdale to Miami, I received an email from Winn Claybaugh, cofounder and dean of Paul Mitchell the School, stating that he wanted to invite me to speak in Costa Mesa, California, so he and his team could hear my persentation. They would

· 187 ·

then determine whether or not I'd get signed to their nonprofit organization, the Andrew Gomez Dream Foundation, which pays guest artists to come into their schools. I was really looking forward to this opportunity because part of my dream was to monetize the gifts God had given me.

I walked into the grand hotel they'd booked for me in Orange County with my black sweatpants on and my hat backwards. The other guests and employees wore their business suits and ties, and I felt completely out of place. In my hotel room, I immediately started preparing myself for the presentation I'd give the next day. I was determined to deliver with excellence. It was my first time in California, and I really wanted to soak up the moment, but at the same time, I wanted to spend time practicing so I could project greatness.

Not long after I arrived, I realized I'd forgotten my phone charger and my phone was drained. I took an Uber to Target to pick up a charger and walked about two miles back to the hotel. The weather was unbelievable and I realized what Day-Day in Next Friday meant when he said, "The air taste different!" The sun was setting as I walked back to the hotel and to feel it radiate off my skin was marvelous. The palms trees swayed in the wind, almost convincing me to uproot my life in Texas to start a new life in Southern California.

The next morning, I took an Uber to Paul Mitchell the School Costa Mesa. My heart was beating fast on the drive because I really didn't know what to expect. As I pulled up to the school, I took my earbuds out and took a deep breath.

The woman at the front desk greeted me with a smile. "You must be Jordan McCook, our guest speaker for today." She directed me to the back office where I would wait until Winn and his staff arrived. I was offered water and snacks to make me feel comfortable. I wasn't uncomfortable, but I didn't know how to show up in that moment. So many thoughts went through my mind about how I should articulate and conduct myself, but in truth, being myself had always worked best.

From around the front desk and down the long hallway, came a physically fit, bald man with a big grin on his face. He was lively and everyone greeted him happily. I thought to myself that this must be Winn. As he entered the room, he greeted me by name with a big smile on his face. We discussed who I was and how I got involved with Paul Mitchell the School and who he was and his involvement with Paul Mitchell.

It was around the holiday season, so we discussed our plans for Thanksgiving and Christmas. He also made me aware that he had a daughter who was five years old, and I bragged about how amazingly cute my one-year-old son was. Our children became our common denominator and made the conversation more relaxed and intimate.

When it was time for me to hit the stage and present, I was ready, but the butterflies in my stomach wouldn't give me a rest. Winn took the stage first to introduce me. "Hello everyone!" he said. "Today is a special day. We have a guest artist all the way from Texas to share with us. I don't know what, but he has been hounding me for quite some time now, and we're all going to be introduced to who he is in a moment. So without further ado, put your hands together for Jordan McCook!"

As I approached the stage, I was tense. I tried to display on the outside the opposite of the feelings running through my body on the inside. As one hundred fifty students looked me in the eye, I got through a very shaky introduction. I felt like a young rap artist seeking to get signed to a label, standing in front of the CEO while he listened to me freestyle. I wanted it to be over. I'd never tensed up onstage like that before, but knowing that Winn Claybaugh and his team were in attendance to hear me speak made the butterflies in my stomach dance like they were at a rave. Nevertheless, I was there for a purpose, and I wasn't going to do anything less than what I came to do. Eventually, my will to succeed overrode my anxiousness and pushed me to deliver with passion and clarity.

Even though I wasn't completely satisfied with my performance, I did the best I could with the nervousness I felt in front of Winn, who was already a high-level speaker. I felt small as he sat in the back of the classroom listening to me speak. After I got off stage, I walked through the crowd. Winn greeted me with a big hug and a smile and said, "You've got what it takes, my friend." I was granted the opportunity to be signed by Paul Mitchell.

* * *

After being on the road consistently and thoroughly enjoying myself, feeling as if I was truly fulfilling my purpose, I made the decision to close down one branch of my business. This was a big decision for me because McCook&Co. Salon Studios was my first storefront business, and I'd truly enjoyed the success I had with it. But it was never a part of my dream. I was spending countless dollars on marketing to fill the suites when it wasn't a passion of mine in the first place. My original intent for that space had been to host my radio show there and have private suites for my clients.

Initially, I wanted to have that space to do a podcast instead of paying for radio show time with the station.

I never even got started with the podcast because, after taking a break for six months, I realized I didn't want to be a radio show personality. I didn't want to be stuck in a studio. I wanted to be on the road, taking stages all over the country and the world. Instead of setting up a recording studio, I'd had the space built into salon suites for beauty professionals.

It was hard letting go because I'd spent about $30,000 in renovations, money I'd saved up, to get all twelve hundred feet of space up to par aesthetically. In the end, it wasn't a waste of money because I learned a lot. I learned what multiple streams of income looks like, the importance of patience in making business decisions, to take the emotion out of business, and to focus on what sells. There was no demand for salon suites in my city. Few stylists were trying to do their own thing, so I was only fully booked for about three months. The common vibe was one of fear. Most stylists and barbers wanted the stability and security of having the owner be responsible for overhead.

My time there had come to an end. It was bittersweet for me, but nevertheless, I was proud of myself and all I'd accomplished. Providing a space for different beauty professionals to work in had created real value. I built many great relationships, and some, if

not all, would be lifetime friendships. All of my ten-
ants had already moved on, which made the transition
smoother. I closed down the space and removed all of
my belongings. The closing was more rewarding than
sad because I'd be able to pursue my passion for speaking without being anchored down by the business. In
December 2018, I closed the doors for good.

CHAPTER 20

Volume 2

The year 2019 was approaching fast and after getting signed by the Andrew Gomez Dream Foundation, I made plans to repeat the "Touching More Hearts Than Heads" tour, but this tour would be volume 2. I was excited to venture to different places and see new cities. I felt called to spread my message as far as I could go because I saw lives that needed to be positively impacted all across America. Since I was finally being paid to speak, it felt right to repeat the tour name with the same heartbeat and passion as volume 1. I felt more credible as a leader and speaker in my industry. This was what I'd always dreamed of, creating a global "Touching More Hearts Than Heads" movement that would free people to be true to themselves and live their best and most authentic life.

THE EVOLUTION OF SELF

It was only appropriate to begin the tour in the great state of Texas in the city I call home, San Antonio. January 3, 2019, was a groundbreaking experience that propelled my speaking career to new heights, my first show as a paid speaker. My mom wasn't able to make it, but family, friends, and clients from around the city were able to see, live and in person, what I'd been doing on the road. It was my first event as an approved speaker for Paul Mitchell, but I hadn't yet met the criteria to get paid. That year, I would do a whole tour on my own dime, making income from merchandise, to build my career. I wasn't getting paid, but this was my dream. I was investing in myself. The money I had spent for the radio show now went into my speaking career. The only way to become a successful speaker was to go hard, and I was willing to do it.

We'd enjoyed our time at Paul Mitchell Houston so much the year before that I decided that's where I'd shoot my special. As the alarm clock went off in my hotel room on October 8, 2019, at six o'clock in the morning, I lay in bed already wide awake. It wasn't nervousness that had woken me, but the anticipation of having an amazing show. For the first time ever, from start to finish, the public would see Jordan McCook in effect.

This was also going to be the first time my mother attended and saw me perform. The anxiety I did feel came from knowing she would be present. After all, I was opening up onstage, in front of strangers, about the traumatic experiences I had growing up in her household. I had no desire to embarrass her, but I believed I could impress people by talking about my accolades or I could positively impact them by talking about my struggles and the journey I'd taken to end up on that stage. I was there to bring impact, inspiration, and influence to every listening ear. I didn't want to hold back.

As I made my way out of the hotel, the wheels in my mind turned. I thought through everything that needed to get done to make the event flow smoothly. From my merchandise table to our production and camera crew to my presentation and performance onstage, it all weighed on me. I had family and friends coming in from out of town and wanted to leave a lasting experience on them. Fortunately, I knew the tasks I'd delegated to each member of my amazing team would get done and we could hit a homerun with this live recording.

I dedicated the speaking engagement to rapper Nipsey Hussle, in honor of his life and contribution to society, and to my mother. Alone in my dressing room, I prayed. "God, use me today. Allow me to be a vessel to say and do whatever you want me to. Help me to bring not only inspiration but impact and a lasting change to people's lives. Touch their hearts, Lord. Move me out the way so they hear you. In Jesus's name I pray. Amen."

The audience poured into the auditorium like ants flowing into a colony. Each seat was filled, and the event was standing room only. In my dressing room, I rehearsed exactly what I would say onstage. With those closest to me standing nearby, I knew this was going to be an epic moment in my speaking career. Heart pounding, palms sweaty, it was time to take the stage and do what God had called me to do—touch more hearts than heads. I was excited for my mother to see me perform, but when it came down to it, I couldn't share many of the stories I would usually tell about growing up in her house. I couldn't be as raw, honest, and open as I normally would be with her there. I censored myself for her sake.

Since I had dedicated the show to her, I wanted to uplift her as much as possible and demonstrate the mindset she'd instilled in me to create and build what I had up to that point. My mother thought it was absolutely phenomenal, and when I was done, I called her onstage and presented her with a bouquet of roses and a gift in a gift bag. She thoroughly enjoyed the experience and constantly repeated how proud of me she was.

For me, the entire event was incredibly stressful. I was glad I delivered with as much passion as I possibly could, but I wasn't pleased with the overall level of authenticity I brought to my performance. I had shied away from that side of the stage where my mother sat in the audience and adjusted my entire presentation not to be offensive to her. In the future, I would be all in every time I spoke.

* * *

In spring of 2019, I was invited by Winn Claybaugh to teach in learning lounges at Caper Paul Mitchell Schools, a national event in Anaheim, California. I immediately accepted the offer and was excited to be back in California, this time speaking at Disneyland. I was dedicated to my dreams and goals, so I was willing to book shows and classes all across America at my own expense. I had never experienced Caper, but I was anticipating an exciting experience.

As the plane skirted the ground in Southern California, the thrill of being able to teach washed over me. My first day there, after checking in to the hotel, I wanted to find a place to eat, and I had been advised by some of my clients back home in Texas to try Roscoe's Chicken and Waffles. So that's exactly what I did. I found the nearest one and took a twenty-minute Uber ride. Dining in by myself wasn't too bad as I stuffed my face with their famous chicken and waffles. I went live

on Instagram to talk to my friends and family and followers about the great experience I was having, and
I guess you could say my Instagram family kept me
company.

I made my way back to the hotel later that evening
to prepare myself for the learning lounges I'd teach
the next day. Up until that moment, I wasn't sure if I
would teach barbering classes or do my normal inspirational speaking, but since I had two class sessions to
lead, I decided to do both. I woke up very early the next
morning and basked in the cool Southern California air
under clear blue skies. But as I went through my clipper
case, I realized I didn't have a cutting cape to use in my
class. I found the nearest Sally's and used the twenty
minutes it took to get there to prepare my mind for the
day. Early in the morning, the streets were busy, and a
lot of the drivers already wore the weight of the work
day on their faces.

At the grand event, thousands of students and
alumni from Paul Mitchell Schools gathered to be edu-
cated, motivated, and inspired by the many celebrity
stylists and barbers and other speakers. All the students
were dressed in black and wore nametags, but my outfit
made it clear that I wasn't a student. I stood out like a
sore thumb in a black-and-white, pinstriped, button-up

shirt with cut-off pants that showed my ankles and bright red vans.

Totally confused as to where I was supposed to be, I looked around for my learning lounge classroom. Hundreds of students from all across the nation swarmed each ballroom, taking pictures and enjoying what the scenery had to offer. Day one was unique because, even though I'd been invited by the dean and cofounder of Paul Mitchell Schools and had a relationship with him, I knew almost no one else there. I felt completely out of place, but I was still excited to teach my class.

Since multiple classes took place at once, I wondered if anyone would bother to sit in my class. Would they know who I was or even be interested to find out? It was my first year as a paid speaker with Paul Mitchell, so I hadn't made a name for myself yet. I feared being forgotten or not being able to deliver the material I'd prepared for the students because no one would show up for my class.

As my time to teach drew nearer, I noticed the celebrity stylist teaching before me had allowed his class to bleed over into my class time—and not just by a few minutes. He'd taken up twenty-five minutes of my hour. I was frustrated because I would barely have been able to pack what I wanted to teach into an hour, let alone thirty-five minutes.

I quickly unpacked my clipper case after finding a model on whom I could perform a very detailed haircut, but in the middle of my class, a lady with a huge entourage of people walking behind her interrupted. "Excuse me, class," she shouted. "I would like to formally introduce you all to Jordan McCook who is one of our inspirational speakers with the Paul Mitchell Schools, and I would like for him to give you a snippet of what takes place in his class." Completely caught off guard, I felt the nervousness rise all over again because I would not be able to provide a snippet of my show and a haircut demonstration in the time I had remaining. "Jordan, these are the owners of every Paul Mitchell school in the nation gathered here with us today."

I wanted the school owners to see how fun, creative, and liberating my class was even though I was in the middle of a haircut demonstration. I had to think on my feet. "On the count of three, I want everybody to give the loudest yell you possibly can. One, two, three!" I screamed. And the students went wild yelling and clapping! The energy of my class went through the roof, but I lost more time. The event coordinator stood in the back, watching the clock, and with five minutes to spare, she told me to shut everything down and make room for the next person's class.

I was frustrated and puzzled because she hadn't done that to the stylist who conducted a class before me. With a third of the haircut I was demonstrating completed and not even speaking a word of inspiration, I made my way into the hallway to finish what I was teaching. Frustrated and sweating profusely, I unpacked all my equipment and carried on the class in a random hallway flooded with people so the remaining few students could see the final product.

After that class, I had about three hours before my next class. I felt so defeated. Rather than hang around, I booked an Uber and took the twenty-minute ride back to my hotel room. I was accustomed to a positive response from people, which I wasn't receiving at this event. Back in my hotel room, I did some self-evaluation and had a talk with myself about what had transpired. It took everything in me not to give up and hide out in my hotel room, but I knew class number two was waiting.

I changed into something lighter because I'd sweated through the clothes I'd worn that morning. Then, I tried to take a nap and relax my mind, but the earlier event ran laps through my brain. I had to make my way back to the school, but this time, I wanted it to be different. Instead of performing a haircut demonstration, I would do what I excelled at and hadn't yet had a chance to do for this audience. I would pour my heart out to the students, touching hearts and minds.

I set up my next class so the students could hear me speak. I told my story and highlighted pivotal points that could make or break you mentally, emotionally, and financially in our industry. This class went over a lot better. It was more intimate, and the response from the students was amazing. Some pulled out their phones to record my talk. Others had tears in their eyes as I shared my life experiences. School owners walked by and heard me speak, and a couple eventually booked me to speak at their schools, Paul Mitchell Delaware and Paul Mitchell Cleveland.

The final day of Caper arrived, the day of the grand stage speaking experience. One by one, five motivational or transformational speakers took the mic and inspired the students with their content. Each of them did a great job, including Tim Storey, a friend of Oprah and mentor to one of the greats, Kanye West. Music blaring, lights flashing, he killed the stage, and the crowd went crazy. Standing in the back of the giant auditorium, I texted Winn: "I've got to meet this guy! Is there any way I can meet Tim Storey?" It was like throwing a coin in a wishing well. I didn't expect to hear back from Winn, but I had to ask. Moments later, I received a text message saying: "Absolutely! Come backstage to the green room."

I was on cloud nine. I had VIP access to meet all the phenomenal speakers who had just graced the stage, but I felt completely out of place again. I wasn't dressed right for the occasion, and I had to make my way through security. People looked at me with a clear question in their eyes: "What are you doing here?"

As I stood around feeling awkward, one of the most impactful speakers, Patrice Washington, host of the Redefining Wealth podcast, approached me. She introduced herself, and I explained to her that I was new to the roster and felt a little lost. I really had no idea what Caper was. She said she didn't know much her first time either and had felt a little out of place, which immediately put me at ease. Patrice was up to speak next, and I stood off to the side and watched from backstage as she captivated the audience. I also introduced myself to her stylist, who explained how she had worked her way up to be a stylist on Steve Harvey's show. It seemed everyone but me had an entourage, but I was just glad to be there, enjoying the moment and connecting with amazing people.

No one knew who I was, and with few exceptions, I didn't know who anybody was or what role they played in the Paul Mitchell organization either. Finally, I followed one of the school owners, who directed me to the back to meet everyone. There I met every speaker, and those meetings opened doors to build relationships and helped me see what was in line for my future.

Evolve Your Self with Leadership

Before there were social media influencers, we had an ancient term that embodied that and more. That term was leadership. In elementary school, a teacher may allow the most well-behaved student to walk to lunch in front of the line as the line leader because this student shows qualities of a leader. Now, I was never that student. I always wanted to be, but I was missing the characteristics of a leader. Instead, I was disruptive. My grades didn't reflect the work of a model student. I was the class clown. It's impossible to be a leader and lead from the back. The leader in any group, community, or organization must lead from the front. This requires exemplifying leadership.

Social media has allowed many people to skip steps. Rather than developing and possessing the qualities of a leader, they gain influence over others through superficial means and live from a place of hypocrisy. The influencers we follow on social media often portray a lifestyle they don't really live. It's easy to impress someone with your accolades, achievements, and the highlights in your life. But few influencers reveal the scars, mistakes, flaws, and overall journey it took to achieve each of those goals. A true leader allows his imperfections to be on display for his audience to learn from.

It's my responsibility as a leader to not lead some with fabricated image of success but to embody what it means to be a real model. Tupac said it best when he said there are so many people playing a role instead of being real models for the generations to come. Leadership isn't just leading when the lights and cameras are on but leading in your private life as well. It's unwise to trust someone who doesn't practice in the dark what they preach in the light. Be very leery of allowing someone to have influence in and over your life who doesn't lead with their imperfections and flaws.

Some people are born with certain leadership skills, but I beg to say those skills can also be taught. Through reading, strategizing, and proper execution you can cultivate the mindset of a leader. It's the constant practice of putting your best foot forward to be the example of not simply what a role model is but, as 2Pac would say, a real model. You will only be as great as the people you make great.

Leaders always have a plan and stay ready so they don't have to get ready. Planning often requires in-depth thought that comes from reading and exercising the power of your mind. The execution requires a relentless and unwavering focus on the pursuit of the goal at hand. True leaders think and behave differently. They're willing to trail-blaze, creating paths that haven't been traveled yet. A leader has an attitude that makes him or her different from followers. You can't be both the leader and the follower on the same journey.

CHAPTER 21

Knowledge
Brings Peace

A quarter of a century, twenty-five years of life, has taught me that a line from the 2014 film Lucy, is just as true in the real world. "Ignorance brings chaos, not knowledge," the character portrayed by Scarlett Johansson says. I couldn't have said it any better myself. Understanding brings a certain level of peace and a calm to the internal unrest we experience as humans, whether it be psychologically, emotionally, or physically. Because people without purpose seek pleasure to numb pain, and the end result is always chaos.

Early in my life, I gave so much time and energy to false pleasures, only to find myself, like a dog chasing its tail, still at the starting line. Your existence begins when you're born, but your life doesn't truly start until you've broken free from the enslavement of any fear that keeps you ignorant to your truest potential.

Shifting my mind to become Self-conscious led to me becoming Self-aware. Through this transformation I've found that every road that leads to heaven leads to a place right inside you. Imagine every fountain of peace, acceptance, validation, identity, success, family that you desire is right inside you. It has been all along, but society has convinced most of us to continually journey and work, searching for answers we already possess. Following what society suggests, you graduate from high school and go get a degree or training to eventually get a good job that provides an honest living so you can raise a family and retire. Too often, we allow our lives to be reduced to somebody else's scale of success.

At the same time, everyone is on this never-ending quest to "find" purpose, whether they're aware of it or not. Many people are asking, "How do I find my purpose?" Others never think to ask themselves this question. Of those who do, most never truly find the answer. Dr. Myles Munroe once said, "The greatest tragedy in life is not death, but a life without purpose." Too many people live out this tragedy.

Why are you here? Why are you alive? Where are you going?

The answers can only be found by going inward. To go beyond existence and dive into a life that can't be confined to society's dictates, dive deep within yourself to become who you truly are. Unlock yourself from the shackles of every limit you've either placed on yourself or have allowed the world to place on you, and you can live a life liberated from mediocrity.

My purpose now is to simply have dominion over every thought, every fear, and every barrier I strive to take them all captive and hold them for ransom, to live and not simply exist. My purpose is to face each of these things, including death, without a drop of fear. What is your purpose?

The awakening of your evolution starts now. There's no turning back. This is your evolution of Self.

ABOUT THE AUTHOR

Jordan McCook is an award-winning master barber, international educator, entrepreneur, and inspirational speaker. He founded McCook&Co., a promotions company, and created the vision for "Touching More Hearts Than Heads," his national speaking tour. As an entrepreneur, Jordan has launched a salon studio while also hosting his popular radio show, featured on 930AM, "The Answer," in San Antonio, TX.

Jordan travels the country as a sponsored Andrew Gomez Dream Foundation speaker. He has appeared on various platforms in the hair industry and at other events where audiences need a message of hope delivered with exuberance and excellence. Drawing from his personal experiences, Jordan puts his life struggles on display to benefit his audience with his heart-felt presentations.

Jordan has a passion for and commitment to pouring into the hearts of any and every listening ear a message of inspiration. His mission is to help each man and woman break free from the enslavement of fear, low self-esteem, insecurities, depression, and anxiety.

Made in the USA
Monee, IL
09 September 2020